SAVING ENDANGERED SPECIES

THE
SPERM WHALE
Help Save This Endangered Species!

Alison Imbriaco

MyReportLinks.com Books

an imprint of

 Enslow Publishers, Inc.

Box 398, 40 Industrial Road
Berkeley Heights, NJ 07922
USA

MyReportLinks.com Books, an imprint of Enslow Publishers, Inc. MyReportLinks®
is a registered trademark of Enslow Publishers, Inc.

Library of Congress Cataloging-in-Publication Data

Imbriaco, Alison.
  The sperm whale : help save this endangered species! / Alison Imbriaco.
      p. cm. — (Saving endangered species)
  Includes bibliographical references and index.
  ISBN-13: 978-1-59845-071-2 (hardcover)
  ISBN-10: 1-59845-071-9 (hardcover)
  1. Sperm whale—Juvenile literature. 2. Sperm whale—Conservation—Juvenile
literature. I. Title.
  QL737.C435I43 2008
  599.5'47—dc22
                                         2006035103

Printed in the United States of America

10 9 8 7 6 5 4 3 2 1

To Our Readers:
Through the purchase of this book, you and your library gain access to the Report Links that specifically
back up this book.
The Publisher will provide access to the Report Links that back up this book and will keep these Report
Links up to date on **www.myreportlinks.com** for five years from the book's first publication date.
We have done our best to make sure all Internet addresses in this book were active and appropriate when
we went to press. However, the author and the Publisher have no control over, and assume no liability for,
the material available on those Internet sites or on other Web sites they may link to.
The usage of the MyReportLinks.com Books Web site is subject to the terms and conditions stated on the
Usage Policy Statement on **www.myreportlinks.com**.
A password may be required to access the Report Links that back up this book. The password is found on
the bottom of page 4 of this book.
Any comments or suggestions can be sent by e-mail to comments@myreportlinks.com or to the address
on the back cover.

Photo Credits: ARKive, p. 49; BBC News, p. 15; © Brandon Cole/ Visuals Unlimited, p. 1, 82; Cetacean
Society International, p. 74; © Chris Bangs — AP Photo/ Guam Variety News, p. 55; Christoph Richter/
SWSS/MMS, p. 108; earthdive.com, p. 44; Enslow Publishers, Inc., p. 5; Environment News Service, p. 66;
© Eric Isselee/Shutterstock.com, pp. 3, 22, 43; © Francois Gohier/ photoresearchers.com, p. 50; IUCN-
World Conservation Union, p. 81; Keep America Beautiful, p. 24; Library of Congress, pp. 59 (Currier &
Ives), 62, 85; Marine Operations Center, Atlantic/NOAA, from the Project GOMEX Sperm Whale survey, p. 52;
Melville.org, p. 12; Monterey Bay Aquarium, p. 28; MyReportLinks.com Books, p. 4; National Marine
Mammal Laboratory/NOAA, p. 26; National Wildlife Magazine, pp. 40, 56; New Bedford Whaling Museum,
p. 17; Newsday Inc., p. 106; NOAA National Marine Fisheries Service, p. 99; NOAA National Marine
Sanctuaries, p. 68; PBS, p. 13, 95; Photos.com, p. 14, 34, 42, 72, 76; © Robert Fullerton/ Shutterstock.com,
p. 19; Rocky Beach, NMML, NOAA Fisheries, SEFSC, pp. 60, 70; Santa Barbara City College, p. 64; Scott
Hill/ NOAA Fisheries SEFSC, p. 54; Sea Shepherd Conservation Society, p. 111; The Acoustic Ecology
Institute, p. 38; The International Whaling Commission, p. 79; The Ocean Alliance, p. 93; The Oceania
Project, p. 31; The Whale Center of New England, p. 96; U.S. Fish & Wildlife Service, p. 30, 115; velocity-
stock.com (J. H. Clark – original), pp. 10–11; Whale and Dolphin Conservation Society, pp. 90, 104; Whales
in Danger, p. 46; Whalesongs.org, p. 36; Woods Hole Oceanographic Institution, p. 92.

Cover Photo: © Brandon Cole / Visuals Unlimited

CONTENTS

MyReportLinks.com Books
Great Books, Great Links, Great for Research!

The Internet sites featured in this book can save you hours of research time. These Internet sites—we call them **"Report Links"**—are constantly changing, but we keep them up to date on our Web site.

When you see this "Approved Web Site" logo, you will know that we are directing you to a great Internet site that will help you with your research.

Give it a try! Type http://www.myreportlinks.com into your browser, click on the series title and enter the password, then click on the book title, and scroll down to the Report Links listed for this book.

The Report Links will bring you to great source documents, photographs, and illustrations. MyReportLinks.com Books save you time, feature Report Links that are kept up to date, and make report writing easier than ever! A complete listing of the Report Links can be found on pages 116–117 at the back of the book.

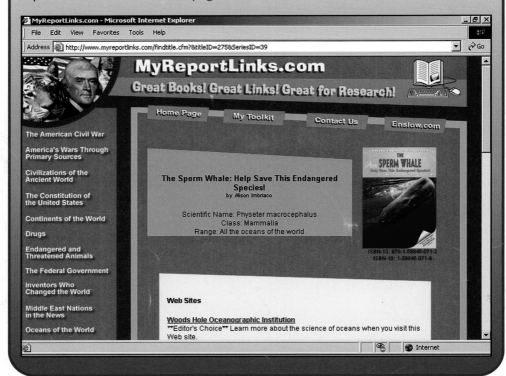

Please see "To Our Readers" on the copyright page for important information about this book, the MyReportLinks.com Web site, and the Report Links that back up this book.

Please enter SWS1335 if asked for a password.

SPERM WHALE
Range Map

ARCTIC OCEAN

ATLANTIC OCEAN

PACIFIC OCEAN

PACIFIC OCEAN

equator

equator

0°

INDIAN OCEAN

N

W   E

S

SOUTHERN OCEAN

SOUTHERN OCEAN

Sperm Whales live in every ocean of the world. Most populations spend winters in warm tropical waters near the equator.

SPERM WHALE FACTS

▶ **Class**
Mammalia

▶ **Order**
Cetacea

▶ **Suborder**
Odontoceti

▶ **Genus and species**
Physeter macrocephalus

▶ **Habitat**
All the oceans of the world

▶ **Estimated population**
Estimates suggest a global population of 360,000.

▶ **Length**
Males grow to a length of 49 to 60 feet (15 to 18 meters); females may grow to almost 40 feet (12 meters).

▶ **Weight**
Males can weigh 35 to 45 tons (32 to 41 metric tons); females can weigh 13 to 15 tons (12 to 14 metric tons).

▶ **Age at Sexual Maturity**
Males are sexually mature at the age of ten, but they usually do not actively take part in breeding until they are in their late twenties. Females are sexually mature by the age of seven to ten.

▶ Gestation

14 to 16 months. Newborn calves weigh approximately 1 ton (907 kilograms) and are 11 to 16 feet (3.4 to 4.9 meters) long.

▶ Physical Description

Sperm whales have blunt, squared-off heads with a single blowhole on the left side. Their heads are almost one third of their total body length and more than one third of their weight. They are usually a dark brownish gray with light streaks, spots, and scratches. The skin on the head is smooth; the skin on the rest of the body has indentations and creases. The dorsal fin is low and rounded and the side flippers are relatively small. The flukes are broad, measuring as much as 15 feet (5 meters) across.

▶ Dives

Deepest dives: to a depth of 65,560 feet (2,000 meters), lasting more than an hour.
Usual dives: to depths of about 1,000 to 2,500 feet (300 to 800 meters), lasting 30 to 45 minutes.

▶ Food

The main source of food is deep-water squid, although they also eat fish, skate, and octopus. A sperm whale eats about 1 ton (907 kilograms) of food a day.

▶ Threats

Reduced numbers and loss of large males and mature females due to past whaling, continued whaling, slow reproduction, ocean pollution, noise pollution, entanglement in fishing nets, ship strikes, and expansion of deep sea fisheries.

"Living cetaceans have an almost unbelievable capacity for enriching the lives of human beings with whom they come in peaceful contact. . . . They have a uniquely universal appeal to the human spirit. They are unmatched invokers of awe. There is a mystique about them that inspires a sense of wonder and exhilaration among persons from all races and nations. . . ."

— Dr. Robbins Barstow,
Cetacean Society International
Director Emeritus, from his
address at the Fourth Annual
"Whales Alive Conference,"
Jan. 1996.

Chapter 1

SPERM WHALES IN DANGER

For the men on the whaling ship *Essex,* November 20, 1820, began as a good day. Whalers often spent weeks looking for sperm whales and seeing none. But on this day, the *Essex* lookout spotted whales.

Crews quickly lowered the small whaling boats that would take them close to the whales so a harpooner could throw the harpoon to attach the whaling boat to a whale. But things did not go well for the boat that carried the first mate. He successfully harpooned a great male sperm whale, but the whale's thrashing tail, known as its flukes, smashed a hole in the wooden boat. The men cut loose from the whale, stuffed cloth in the hole, and managed to get back to the ship. The first mate hauled the broken boat aboard and began to repair it.

Suddenly the whalers saw the huge, wounded whale swimming directly toward the ship, beating the water with its flukes to gain speed. The whale rammed the ship, knocking everyone to the deck. When the whale rushed the ship again, it damaged the ship so badly that the crew had to abandon it. The whalers left the ruined ship in three small whaling boats. The eight men who survived spent months on the open ocean in the little boats. They only survived by eating companions who had died. The *Essex* was the first whaling ship to be sunk by a whale, but it would not be the last.[1]

▶ **Moby Dick**

Some years later, the first mate's son shared his father's story with another young whaler named

Created in 1813 by artist J. H. Clark, this painting shows a fairly early portrayal of whaling. In this scene, a man at the bow of the boat is not throwing the harpoon by hand, but firing a harpoon gun.

Herman Melville. In 1851, Melville published *Moby Dick,* which was based on the story of the *Essex.* Melville depicted the white whale Moby Dick as a vengeful monster bent on destruction. The sperm whale, according to Melville, was "most monstrous and most mountainous! . . . clothed with such portentousness of unconscious power, that his very panics are more to be dreaded than his most fearless and malicious assaults!"[2] *Moby*

Dick describes in detail what it was like to be a whaler in the 1800s, when men set sail in wooden ships in pursuit of sperm whales. The ships were often gone for years at a time—and some never returned. Violent ocean storms could send them to the bottom of the ocean. But the promise of riches drew the whalers around the tip of South America to the wide Pacific Ocean.

▶ The Sperm Whale's Wealth

Carved drawings in South Korea indicate that people used boats and spears to hunt whales about six thousand years ago.[3] The first whalers probably killed whales for food. Eventually, though, people found another important use for

The Life and Works of Herman Melville - Microsoft Internet Explorer

File   Edit   View   Favorites   Tools   Help

Address http://www.melville.org/   Go

The Life and Works of Herman Melville

The Life and Works of Herman Melville is a publication dedicated to disseminating information about Herman Melville on the Internet and the World Wide Web. Another valuable Internet resource is *Ishmail*, an electronic mailing list devoted to the discussion of Melville, his works, and other related subjects.

The Life and Works of Herman Melville

Learn more about the nineteenth-century American novelist Herman Melville, whose greatest work, *Moby Dick,* is a tale about the hunt to kill a "great white whale."

Access this Web site from http://www.myreportlinks.com

whales. All whales have a thick layer of fat, called blubber, under their skin. At some point, people learned that if they cooked the blubber through a process called rendering, it would produce oil. This oil was valuable because it could be used in lamps.

For thousands of years, people relied on oil lamps and candles to bring light into darkness. They filled containers (like the one Aladdin rubbed to summon his genie) with oil pressed from olives and other plants. They made candles with animal fat and beeswax. People needed to press many olives to obtain the oil they now could get from one whale.

▶ Sperm Whales Discovered

Sperm whales had nothing to fear from early whalers since the whales live in the deepest parts of the ocean, far from land and out of the reach of small ships.

In 1712, according to legend, a Yankee, or New England, whaling ship sailing near Nantucket (an island south of Cape Cod, Massachusetts) was blown off course and came upon some sperm whales. The whalers killed one, dragged it back to shore, and discovered the supply of oil that sperm whales carry in their enormous heads.

Sperm whales' heads are huge—about one third of their total length and more than one third

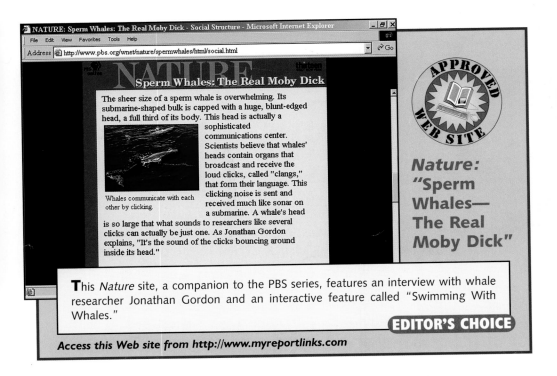

NATURE: Sperm Whales: The Real Moby Dick - Social Structure - Microsoft Internet Explorer

File   Edit   View   Favorites   Tools   Help

Address   http://www.pbs.org/wnet/nature/spermwhales/html/social.html

Sperm Whales: The Real Moby Dick

The sheer size of a sperm whale is overwhelming. Its submarine-shaped bulk is capped with a huge, blunt-edged head, a full third of its body. This head is actually a sophisticated communications center. Scientists believe that whales' heads contain organs that broadcast and receive the loud clicks, called "clangs," that form their language. This clicking noise is sent and received much like sonar on a submarine. A whale's head is so large that what sounds to researchers like several clicks can actually be just one. As Jonathan Gordon explains, "It's the sound of the clicks bouncing around inside its head."

Whales communicate with each other by clicking.

Nature: "Sperm Whales— The Real Moby Dick"

This *Nature* site, a companion to the PBS series, features an interview with whale researcher Jonathan Gordon and an interactive feature called "Swimming With Whales."

EDITOR'S CHOICE

Access this Web site from http://www.myreportlinks.com

The head of a sperm whale is squarish and its blowhole is located to the forward-left side of it. Water shoots forward from its blowhole rather than straight up out of the hole as in other whales.

of their total mass. The head of a large male can be almost twenty feet (six meters) long and weigh fifteen tons (fourteen metric tons)! Inside sperm whales' heads are two "containers" filled with what the whalers called oil. One of the two containers holds a liquid wax that the whalers named spermaceti oil. This "oil" burned brighter and cleaner than any other oil and made the finest candles. Trade in spermaceti oil made people rich.

Sperm whales sometimes carry another prize. Sperm whales eat squid, and they swallow squid beaks, which can irritate their intestines. The whales produce a substance called ambergris to coat the squid beaks. People sometimes found ambergris floating in the ocean and learned that the strange substance was the best fixative for perfume, keeping it from evaporating. Ambergris is very valuable. No one knew the substance came from sperm whales until whalers found it in the intestines of whales they had killed. Ambergris provided one more reason to hunt sperm whales.

By the 1800s, shipbuilders were building larger ships with three masts and square sails that sailed around the world in pursuit of sperm whales. Whaling was a dangerous business, but the promise of wealth inspired many whalers to risk their lives in pursuit of whales. In 1841,

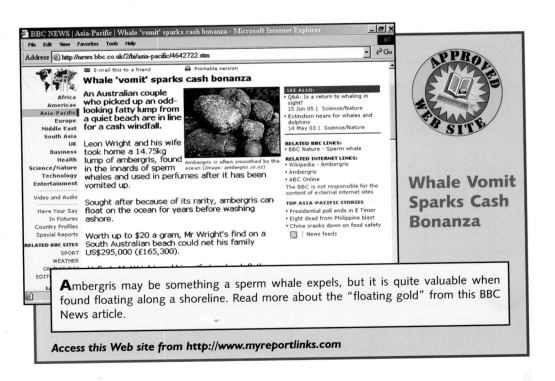

Ambergris may be something a sperm whale expels, but it is quite valuable when found floating along a shoreline. Read more about the "floating gold" from this BBC News article.

Access this Web site from http://www.myreportlinks.com

seventy-five ships sailed from New Bedford, Massachusetts, to search for sperm whales. By 1857 the New Bedford whaling ships employed more than ten thousand men.[4]

▶ Changes in the Whaling Industry

Yankee whaling hit its peak in the 1840s. In 1843, whalers brought in about 5 million gallons (almost 20 million liters) of sperm oil.[5] Between 1792 and 1913, Yankee whalers killed an esti- mated thirty-six thousand sperm whales.[6] Whalers from other countries also hunted sperm whales, but the Yankee whalers were the greatest threat to the whales.

For several reasons, the hunt for sperm whales began to taper off about 1850. One reason was simply that large sperm whales became harder to find. In addition, the discovery of petroleum in Pennsylvania in 1859 provided a substitute for whale oil in the form of kerosene. And in 1879, the electric lamp was invented.

Between 1880 and 1946, whalers pursued other whales, and few sperm whales died at the hands of whalers. But as other whale species began to disappear, whalers turned to sperm whales again. People had found new uses for spermaceti oil. It was used in the manufacture of products as varied as steel, textiles, and soap. Treating the sperm whale oil with sulfur makes it

During the nineteenth century, New Bedford, Massachusetts, was known as the whaling capital of the world. Find more information on New England's rich whaling history at the Web site of the **New Bedford Whaling Museum.**

a superior lubricant, so it was used in automatic transmissions and high-altitude instruments.

When the hunt for sperm whales resumed, the whale faced a very different enemy. By the 1940s, whaling had become much more efficient. Steam-powered whaleboats with cannon that fired exploding harpoons left little hope for the whales. Hundreds of thousands of sperm whales were killed in just a few decades. In 1964 alone, whalers killed more than twenty-nine thousand sperm whales.[7]

How Many Sperm Whales?

No one knows how many whales there were before the days of whaling, and no one knows how many whales are alive today. The deep-diving animals are hard to find, and following them is just as difficult because they are constantly on the move. According to the rough estimates that many researchers accept today, the oceans were home to about 1.1 million whales before the 1800s. Today about 360,000 whales inhabit the oceans. (By comparison, the population of Columbus, Ohio, is about 730,000, just over twice the number of whales spread out in the world's oceans.)[8]

A population of 360,000 might seem plenty large enough to keep the species healthy. However, sperm whales seem to be recovering slowly. One reason is simply that sperm whales reproduce slowly. Another reason may be that whalers killed the largest whales—the breeding males and mature females. The disproportionate loss of these large whales may have disrupted the social structures that help sperm whales survive.

New Threats

In 1982 the International Whaling Commission (IWC) decided that commercial whaling should come to a halt, with nearly all whaling ceasing by 1986. Whaling is no longer the threat it once was in the mid-1900s, although it continues in Norway,

Japan, and Iceland. However, the oceans have changed, and whales now confront other dangers.

Fishing nets sometimes trap whales and may cause them to drown. Large ships sometimes collide with whales and kill them. Loud noises from Navy sonar, underwater oil exploration, and other sources may disrupt the behavior of animals that rely on hearing to find their food. Man-made noise

Of all the great cetaceans, the sperm whale is the deepest diver and can remain underwater for more than an hour. This photo shows the low, rounded dorsal fin of a whale beginning its dive.

may also be making it difficult for whales to hunt and to communicate with one another.

Human Impact on Whales

Perhaps the greatest threat to whales and all marine life is pollution in the ocean. People have dumped millions of tons of waste directly into the ocean, and rivers continue to carry toxic chemicals to the sea. We continue to read about oil spills causing miles of blackened shoreline and hundreds of dead birds, mammals, and fish. However, the World Wildlife Fund reports that 80 percent of marine pollution comes from land-based sources such as garbage, industrial waste, and fertilizers that flow into the oceans from storm drains and rivers.[9]

The toxic chemicals pouring into the ocean become concentrated in whales' bodies. The smallest organisms in the ocean absorb the poisons and are then eaten by fish, which are eaten by larger fish. The effects of pollution increase at each step of the food chain. Since sperm whales are at the top of the food chain, they consume the most concentrated poison. Then their thick layers of blubber store the toxic chemicals.

Another very serious threat to all marine life is global warming. Melting glaciers are changing the oceans in ways that scientists are only beginning to understand. One change that scientists have already noticed is that carbon dioxide, one of the main culprits in global warming, is making the oceans more acidic. The high levels of CO_2 may kill small organisms at the bottom of the ocean's food chain, which would in turn have a deadly ripple effect on the larger fish and animals that rely on those organisms for food.

What You Can Do to Help Whales

The first step toward helping an endangered species is learning about it. You are already taking that first step as you read this book. You can learn more by following the links in this book to Web sites with information about sperm whales and their habitat, which is all the world's oceans. As you learn about sperm whales, share what you learn with people around you. Sperm whales are fascinating animals!

A great way to learn about whales is to watch them. Since sperm whales live in deep parts of the ocean, you would have to travel to the Caribbean Islands or other distant locations to see them. If you live close to the Atlantic or Pacific Ocean, though, whale-watching tours that take people close to other whales might be nearby. Tours from New England take people to the feeding grounds of humpback, right, and minke whales. Tours from the Pacific Coast find gray whales along their migration route. It is a thrilling event to be able to see any whale species, and the more you learn about whales in general, the better able you will be to talk about sperm whales in particular.

Whether you live close to the ocean or in the middle of the country, you can help prevent ocean pollution, one of the greatest threats to whales today. One way to help prevent ocean pollution is

▲ There is much controversy over whether whale watching should be legal or not. Among the pros and cons of the debate is the issue of money. While tours provide income for people and communities and in turn protect the species, tour operators may be tempted to disrupt the whales by coming too close to them.

simply to pick up litter, especially anything made of plastic, so it will not find its way into rivers that will carry it to the ocean. Plastic does not disintegrate for a very long time. A plastic bag left in a picnic area may end up in a whale's stomach years later! (Do you think something as small as a plastic bag could not harm an animal as large as a whale? Biologists performed an autopsy on a sperm whale that died of starvation and found a party balloon blocking its digestive system.)

You might talk to your teacher about helping your class "adopt" an area where you and your classmates would get together regularly to pick up trash. Many states have "Adopt-a-Highway" programs. Or you might adopt a park or playground in your community. Picking up trash can be fun when you do it with friends! You can also go to **www.myreportlinks.com** and click on the link to the Keep America Beautiful Web site for more ideas about how you and your family or class can clean up litter.

▶ Learn About Recycling

Recycling has already reduced the amount of garbage we need to dispose of, but good programs can be made better. Learn about the recycling program in your community.

You might start by visiting your community's recycling center. What materials does it accept,

Keep America Beautiful The Nation's Largest Community Improvement Network - Microsoft Internet Ex...

File   Edit   View   Favorites   Tools   Help

Address http://www.kab.org/getinvolved.asp?id=202&rid=203

The Nation's Largest
★ **Community Improvement**
Network

Contact Us

About Us   Our Programs   Our Network   Partnerships   Media Center   Get Involved

Get Involved
Do Your Part
Donate Now
Become an Affiliate
Find an Affiliate Near You
Become a Sponsor
Ideas for Local Communities
Ideas for Business

More *about...*

Order your family
stewardship kit today!

Find a Keep America Beautiful
affiliate near you for more
specific information on how you
can get involved.

Donate to Keep America
Beautiful.

Do Your Part

Personal responsibility is the hallmark of Keep America
Beautiful's work—Each of us can make a difference!

Keep America Beautiful is a nonprofit organization that works with schools and communities across the United States to reduce litter and waste in the environment. On the group's Web site, learn how you can get involved and help to prevent ocean pollution by cleaning up litter.

and what happens to those materials after they reach the recycling center? Does your community provide a way to dispose of hazardous and toxic material, such as oil used in cars? Then look at how much of the garbage that could be recycled is actually going to the recycling center. Perhaps you and your friends or classmates can think of ways to encourage people in your community to pay more attention to recycling. Or you might look at ways your community can make recycling easier for people and then share your ideas with local elected officials.

Your family can make recycling more profitable for the companies involved in recycling by choosing products made from recycled material. Labels on some products, such as paper towels, will tell you whether the product is made from recycled paper.

▶ Chemical Pollution

Plastic is not the only harmful substance finding its way into the oceans. Rain carries fertilizer from neighborhood lawns and large farms into rivers and then into the oceans. If your family takes care of a lawn, ask your parents if they would try organic fertilizer. You might also discuss composting vegetable garbage to use in your garden or lawn.

Your family can also influence the use of fertilizers on large farms by choosing to buy organic food. Farmers have been afraid to stop using harmful fertilizers, thinking they would not be able to make enough money without the fertilizers. By choosing to buy organic foods, your family can help make environmentally friendly farming profitable.

The toxic chemicals draining into the ocean might include the shampoo you use. Many shampoos and other personal-hygiene products contain chemicals that are harmful to marine life. Look at the ingredients in the products you use, and do some research to learn more about them. You

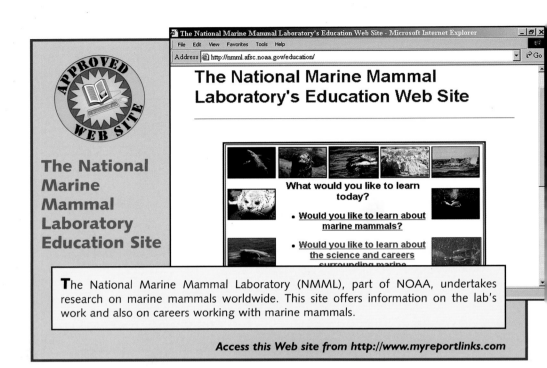

The National Marine Mammal Laboratory's Education Web Site - Microsoft Internet Explorer

File   Edit   View   Favorites   Tools   Help

Address   http://nmml.afsc.noaa.gov/education/   Go

The National Marine Mammal Laboratory's Education Web Site

The National Marine Mammal Laboratory Education Site

What would you like to learn today?

- Would you like to learn about marine mammals?

- Would you like to learn about the science and careers surrounding marine

The National Marine Mammal Laboratory (NMML), part of NOAA, undertakes research on marine mammals worldwide. This site offers information on the lab's work and also on careers working with marine mammals.

Access this Web site from http://www.myreportlinks.com

might choose to buy shampoo and other products from a health-food store.

▶ A Price to Pay

Unfortunately, products that do not harm the environment, such as many sold in health-food stores and other places, are often more expensive than mass-produced ones. In part, that is because many industries do not want to change the products they manufacture to protect animals, such as marine mammals, because it would cost more to do so. Those costs would then be passed on to the consumer—you, your friends, and your family— and you would probably choose to buy cheaper items. Many of those goods, unfortunately, are manufactured without any thought to their lasting effect on people, plants, and wildlife. If we truly want to save sperm whales and other endangered species, we need to be willing to pay the price of goods produced by "green," or environmentally conscious, industries.

What's for Dinner?

Many Americans are choosing to eat more fish because of the health benefits fish offer. However, overfishing has already resulted in fewer fish in the ocean. Fishermen trying to make a living in overfished oceans may use methods that harm the ocean floor and result in huge amounts of "bycatch." The term *bycatch* refers to unwanted fish and marine animals that are caught in fishing gear and later discarded. Bycatch might include young fish too small to be sold that will never grow up to reproduce. Bycatch also includes seals, whales, and seabirds.

Your family can encourage responsible fishing methods by choosing fish carefully when shopping for it. The Monterey Bay Aquarium's Web site includes a seafood guide that suggests which fish to buy and which fish to avoid to support responsible fishing. For example, the Atlantic cod population is already so depleted that the species may soon disappear. In addition, Atlantic cod live near the

Monterey Bay Aquarium: Seafood Watch Program

This Monterey Bay Aquarium site offers downloadable pocket guides aimed at educating consumers about the fish they buy, since those choices affect other fish and marine life in general. It also offers ways you can become active in saving our oceans and the life in them.

Access this Web site from http://www.myreportlinks.com

ocean floor. Fishermen often use bottom trawling, dragging large nets across the ocean floor to catch cod. Trawling damages undersea habitats and results in large quantities of bycatch.

Some fish sold in stores were raised in fish farms. While fish farms eliminate the problem of bycatch, they can cause other problems. For example, farmed salmon are crowded in pens in coastal areas, and the waste from the pens flows directly into the ocean. In the crowded pens, the fish are susceptible to disease, so salmon farmers may use antibiotics and pesticides. Traces of both may be in the fish when it is eaten. In addition, it actually takes more wild fish to feed farmed salmon than the farms produce.

Cleaner Air Means Cleaner Oceans

Every time you choose to ride your bicycle instead of riding in a car you are helping whales and everything else that lives in the ocean. The carbon dioxide from automobile emissions becomes part of the atmosphere, and some of it is absorbed by the ocean, making the water more acidic. Carbon dioxide also contributes to global warming, which is changing the ocean in ways that scientists are only beginning to understand.

The idea that carpooling in the United States can help whales off the coast of New Zealand may seem like quite a stretch. However, every effort to reduce automobile emissions is a step toward a healthier ocean. Find out what your community does to promote carpooling, and then think of more ways to encourage people to share rides.

Be Politically Active

Laws passed at all levels of government can affect the future of sperm whales. Learn more about laws and congressional acts aimed at preserving our environment. You might start with the Clean Water Act and Clean Air Act. Both have a direct impact on your own environment as well as the health of the oceans.

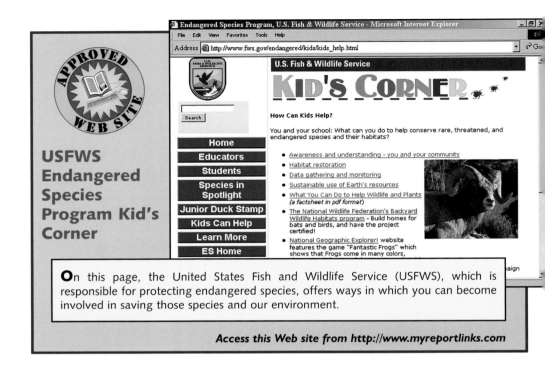

USFWS
Endangered
Species
Program Kid's
Corner

U.S. Fish & Wildlife Service

KID'S CORNER

How Can Kids Help?

You and your school: What can you do to help conserve rare, threatened, and endangered species and their habitats?

- Awareness and understanding - you and your community
- Habitat restoration
- Data gathering and monitoring
- Sustainable use of Earth's resources
- What You Can Do to Help Wildlife and Plants (a factsheet in pdf format)
- The National Wildlife Federation's Backyard Wildlife Habitats program - Build homes for bats and birds, and have the project certified!
- National Geographic Explorer! website features the game "Fantastic Frogs" which shows that Frogs come in many colors,

Home
Educators
Students
Species in Spotlight
Junior Duck Stamp
Kids Can Help
Learn More
ES Home

On this page, the United States Fish and Wildlife Service (USFWS), which is responsible for protecting endangered species, offers ways in which you can become involved in saving those species and our environment.

Access this Web site from http://www.myreportlinks.com

Two additional acts passed in the early 1970s also help sperm whales. The Marine Mammal Protection Act makes it illegal to harm or kill whales, with a few exceptions. The Endangered Species Act of 1973 also makes harming or killing whales illegal, and it provides for research to develop a recovery plan for every endangered species.

Industries and individuals often challenge these laws. Industries may fear that changes required by the laws will put them out of business. While it is appropriate that laws be continually reviewed, large industries that can hire lobbyists may influence politicians in ways that are not good for the general public. The Endangered Species Act, especially, is often in danger itself.

The federal government can also help sperm whales and the oceans by persuading other countries to protect whales and to stop polluting the oceans. Your government can choose to use economic sanctions, which means it threatens to stop another country from selling goods in the United States. Imposing sanctions can harm the economy of the sanctioned country and the economy of the United States, so sanctions should not be used unless necessary. In the past, the United States has used the threat of sanctions to convince countries to stop killing whales.

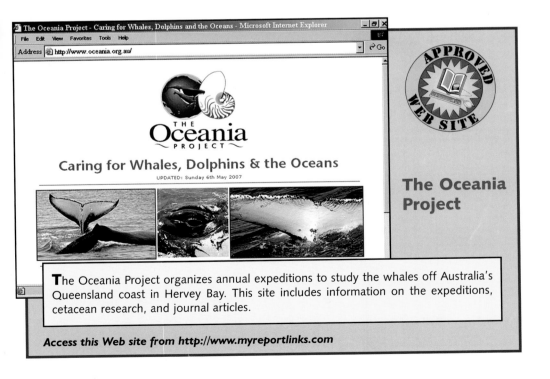

The Oceania Project

The Oceania Project organizes annual expeditions to study the whales off Australia's Queensland coast in Hervey Bay. This site includes information on the expeditions, cetacean research, and journal articles.

Access this Web site from http://www.myreportlinks.com

Although you cannot vote yet, you can influence those who do vote. Pay attention to the news, and listen for political debates about the environment and proposed laws to protect the environment. Many of the Web sites of environmental organizations keep readers up to date about laws and issues that affect the environment and endangered species. Discuss these issues with your friends and with adults. Discussions will help you understand the issues and will remind others how important the issues are.

Find out who your elected officials are and how they vote on environmental issues. After you have learned about the issues, you can work with your friends or classmates to write letters to elected officials encouraging them to pay attention to the issues important to you.

As you learn about sperm whales, the ocean, and laws to protect both, you may have more ideas about ways to help save sperm whales. The important thing to remember is that if you care, you *can* make a difference in a species' chance of survival.

Chapter 2 ▶

HUNTERS IN THE OCEAN DEPTHS

People have been killing sperm whales for centuries, but even today marine biologists, scientists who study life in the ocean, have many unanswered questions about the giant ocean-dwelling mammal.

▶ What the Whalers Saw

Some facts are obvious. Men who sailed in wooden ships to hunt whales certainly noticed that sperm whales were often larger than the small boats the harpooners used to get close to them. The whalers also observed behavior that seemed strange to them. Sometimes after they harpooned and wounded a sperm whale, other whales would not swim away from the danger. Instead the whales would stay with their wounded companion "to the last moment, or until they are wounded themselves," wrote one nineteenth-century whaler.[1]

Early whalers were especially interested in sperm whales because the species, with its squared-off heads, did not look like other whale species. Whalers knew the huge heads hold two large "barrels," one on top of the other. These barrel-like containers are made of muscle, and they contain tissue soaked in a substance the whalers called oil.

Although the whalers had no idea why sperm whales carried containers of oil in their heads, they quickly learned that the oil in the top container made the finest smokeless candles. They called the waxy liquid in the top container spermaceti oil. The oil in the lower container had less

▲ *This woodcut depicts a sperm whale blowing near a sailing ship. The print was first published by Olaus Magnus in 1555.*

commercial value, so whalers named it "the junk." Today, scientists still refer to the spermaceti organ and the junk.

The Sperm Whale's Nose

When scientists looked more closely at the containers in a sperm whale's head, they noticed that the whale's nasal passages went through them. The containers seemed to be part of a giant nose. Like other whales, sperm whales breathe air through a blowhole on top of their heads. A sperm whale's blowhole is on the left side of its head, and an air tube, the left nasal passage, runs from the blowhole through the top container and directly to the whale's lungs. The right nasal passage takes a more interesting route. It runs between the upper and lower containers and forms air sacs at the front and back of them. A muscle that works like a valve opens to let air into the front air sac.

Examining sperm whales' air passages did not immediately explain why the whales carried two enormous barrels of oil-soaked tissue in their heads. Early whalers saw the whales using their oversized heads as battering rams and thought that might be the reason for the oil.

Finally, in 1972, two scientists suggested that the spermaceti organ, the junk, the air sacs, and the odd valvelike muscle work together in a wonderful biosonar system.[2] Whales use their built-in sonar for echolocation, which is a way of using sound to find prey in the dark depths of the ocean.

The Odontocetes

Sperm whales are not the only whales that use echolocation to locate prey. Sperm whales are members of a group of whales and dolphins (cetaceans) called odontocetes. This group includes beluga whales, all dolphins (including killer whales, which are actually dolphins), bottlenose whales, porpoises, and others. All odontocetes have teeth of some kind. Sperm whales, the

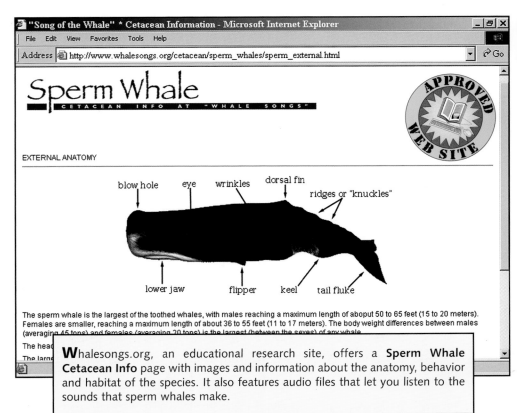

Whalesongs.org, an educational research site, offers a **Sperm Whale Cetacean Info** page with images and information about the anatomy, behavior and habitat of the species. It also features audio files that let you listen to the sounds that sperm whales make.

largest of all odontocetes, have visible teeth only on their lower jaw. (They have some unerupted teeth in their upper jaw.) These visible teeth, up to fifty of them, can grow up to ten inches (twenty-five centimeters) and weigh over two pounds (one kilogram) each.[3] The teeth in the lower jaw fit into sockets in the upper jaw.

Odontocetes make clicking sounds and then listen to the echoes to navigate and to locate prey. Most odontocetes also make tonal sounds, although sperm whales do not. The odontocetes produce the clicks in their heads, in the nasal passages. Then they focus the sound into a narrow beam, like a flashlight beam in a dark room. The beam of sound bounces off objects and returns as an echo. Echolocation is efficient underwater because sound travels about five times faster through water than it does through air.

▶ Specialized Hearing

In order to get information from the echoes of their clicks, the sperm whales need to hear the echoes. They do not have ears on the outside of their heads the way other mammals do, but like all mammals, they have inner ears containing an organ called a cochlea, which sends sound signals to the brain. Air-filled sacs around the cochlea may help them determine what direction a sound comes from.

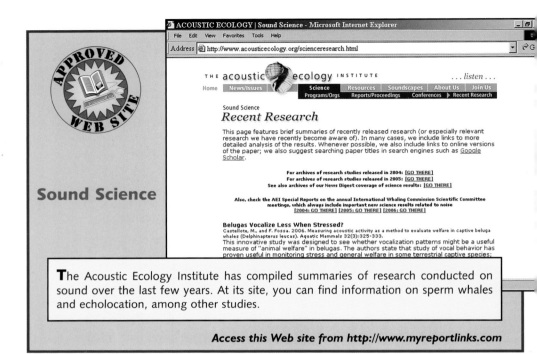

The Acoustic Ecology Institute has compiled summaries of research conducted on sound over the last few years. At its site, you can find information on sperm whales and echolocation, among other studies.

Access this Web site from http://www.myreportlinks.com

However, sound carried by water passes through the whales' bodies, which themselves are mostly water. Something needs to "catch" the sound waves and send them to the whales' ears. Scientists believe a fat-filled channel in the lower jaw does just that. Scientists have also learned that whales' ear bones are the densest bones on Earth,[4] and these bones may stop sound waves that then cause tissue around the bones to vibrate.

Scientists do not fully understand how sperm whales hear, just as they do not completely understand how the whales make and use the clicks. What they have learned, though, reveals that the whales' use of echolocation is amazing.

▶ Sperm Whale Clicks

The clicks of most odontocetes are high-frequency, high-pitched sounds. The frequency of a sound wave is the number of vibrations it makes in one second. A high-pitched sound wave has a short wavelength, which gets shorter as the pitch gets higher.

Sperm whales, with their huge sound-producing organ, send out low-frequency clicks with longer wavelengths that travel much farther. In fact, sperm whale clicks can travel up to six miles (ten kilometers) in the water. And they are very loud—the loudest sounds made by any mammal. One biologist said that the whales' clicks can be about as loud as a rifle shot three feet (one meter) from one's ear.[5]

As whales dive in search of food, their clicks are evenly spaced, with half a second to a full second between each click. Sometimes the clicks change and become so close together that they sound like an old door creaking on rusty hinges. Scientists think the whales creak when they have found food and are closing in on it.

Sperm whales sometimes creak when they are at the surface of the water to scan objects, such as the boats used by marine biologists—or the biologists themselves when they are in the water. A biologist who was in the water with sperm whales said he could actually feel the echolocation clicks hitting his body.[6]

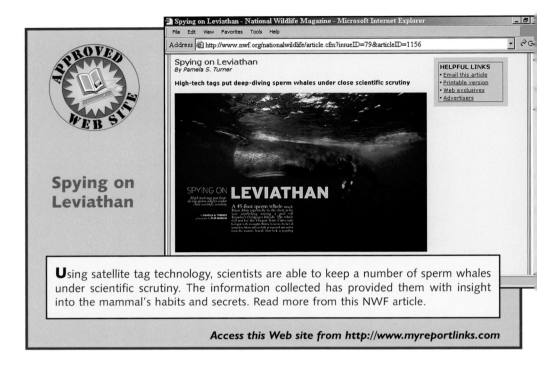

Spying on Leviathan - National Wildlife Magazine - Microsoft Internet Explorer

File   Edit   View   Favorites   Tools   Help

Address   http://www.nwf.org/nationalwildlife/article.cfm?issueID=79&articleID=1156

Spying on Leviathan
By Pamela S. Turner

High-tech tags put deep-diving sperm whales under close scientific scrutiny

HELPFUL LINKS
• Email this article
• Printable version
• Web exclusives
• Advertisers

Spying on Leviathan

Using satellite tag technology, scientists are able to keep a number of sperm whales under scientific scrutiny. The information collected has provided them with insight into the mammal's habits and secrets. Read more from this NWF article.

Access this Web site from http://www.myreportlinks.com

▶ Diving Deep

Echolocation is useful to sperm whales because they hunt where there is little light. Sperm whales dive deep into the ocean in search of their preferred food, squid. Average dives take the whales to depths of almost 1,000 to almost 2,000 feet (300 to 600 meters). However, sperm whales can dive to depths over 6,600 feet (2,000 meters).[7] The only other mammals that dive as deep as sperm whales are elephant seals and some beaked whales.

The ocean is very different a thousand feet below the surface. The light becomes dimmer in this "twilight" zone. At 3,000 feet (914 meters) below the surface, the water is completely dark, except for occasional light from bioluminescent fish that give off light made in their bodies. No plants live at this depth, and the temperature is cool, about 36°F (2°C).

The pressure is also different. The atmospheric pressure doubles every thirty-three feet (ten meters) down in ocean water. At a depth of about sixteen hundred feet (five hundred meters), the pressure is fifty times the pressure at the surface.[8]

▶ Champion Divers

Whales have adapted to the demands of deep diving. They can hold their breath for a very long time. Average dives keep sperm whales under water for about thirty to forty-five minutes, although the whales can hold their breath for more than an hour at a time. Whales use the oxygen in their bodies efficiently as they dive. Their bodies direct oxygen where it is needed most—to the heart and brain—while less oxygen goes to the rest of their bodies. Their heart rate slows at the same time.

As the whales descend deeper, their lungs and jointed ribs collapse so there is less outside pressure on the air in their lungs. Compared to humans, whales store more oxygen in their muscles and less in their lungs. In addition, whales have a greater proportion of red blood cells, which carry oxygen. Red blood cells make up less than 3 percent of a person's body volume, but about 12 percent of a sperm whale's body volume.[9]

Sperm whales begin their dives by arching their backs and lifting their powerful flukes above the water. For about fifteen minutes, they swim straight down at a rate of about three and a half miles per hour (five and a half kilometers per hour). The whales' flukes propel them through the water. Like all cetaceans, whales move their flukes up and down rather than side to side as fish do.

Between dives, a sperm whale usually spends seven to ten minutes on the surface, breathing through a blowhole on the left side of its head. Water vapor makes the exhaled breaths look like a bushy spray.

Before a sperm whale begins its dive, it heaves its triangular flukes out of the water.

▲ *Between dives, sperm whales release more than fifty blows while resting on the water's surface.*

▶ The Whale's Prey

About 75 percent of a sperm whale's time is spent diving deep and then breathing at the surface. Whales dive day and night. They need to dive often because they need to eat great quantities of food. One biologist estimated that each day, full-grown males need a ton and a half of food while full-grown females require almost half a ton. At that rate, sperm whales eat about as much each year as humans take annually from the ocean.[10]

Fortunately for people, whales prefer squid, which many people do not like. Squid range in size from 3.5 ounces (100 grams) to almost 900 pounds (400 kilograms). Although they prefer squid, sperm whales also eat a wide variety of other creatures, from sharks to crabs, that live in the dark depths of the ocean.

▶ Cousins of Cows?

Whales have developed in many specialized ways in order to dive deep into the ocean and use echolocation to find food. This evolution is especially remarkable because whales are mammals. They evolved from a wolf-sized land animal that was also an ancestor of cows and pigs.

Fossils indicate that this land animal began to hunt in the oceans about 50 million years ago, after the giant reptiles had disappeared. During the next 15 million years, the ancestors of whales evolved specialized characteristics that allowed the whales to live in the water. One of the most important developments was the evolution of the ear. By 40 million years ago, ancestors of today's

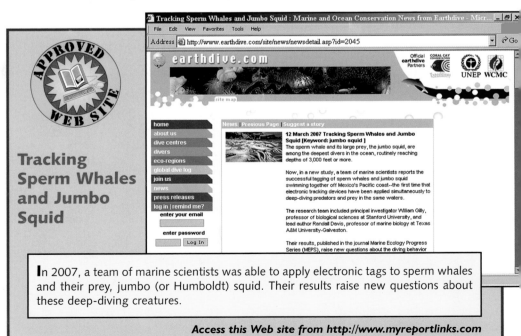

Tracking Sperm Whales and Jumbo Squid

In 2007, a team of marine scientists was able to apply electronic tags to sperm whales and their prey, jumbo (or Humboldt) squid. Their results raise new questions about these deep-diving creatures.

Access this Web site from http://www.myreportlinks.com

cetaceans had developed air sacs around the inner ear to aid in underwater hearing.[11]

Total Makeover

As whales' ancestors gradually adapted to life in the water, their appearance changed completely. Front legs became flippers, which helped the whales steer, and hind legs disappeared. Inside the flippers, bones similar to wrist and finger bones serve as reminders that whales' distant ancestors did not look like whales.[12]

As the ancestors spent more time chasing fish, their tails grew strong to support powerful flukes that propel the whales through the water. Their nostrils moved from the front of the face to the top of the head to make breathing in the water easier.

Whales' skeletons changed, too. Water holds the whales up, so they do not need strong bones to keep them upright. Their bones became lighter and filled with oil to help them stay afloat rather than sinking to the bottom.

What Sperm Whales Look Like

Because of *Moby Dick,* most people picture something that looks like a sperm whale when they think of a whale. In fact, sperm whales look very different from other whales. Sperm whales are the only whales with huge, squared-off heads. The skin covering the spermaceti organ is smooth, but

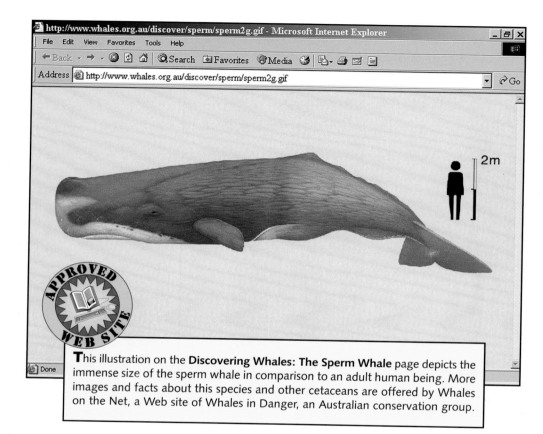

http://www.whales.org.au/discover/sperm/sperm2g.gif - Microsoft Internet Explorer

File   Edit   View   Favorites   Tools   Help

← Back • → • ⊗ ⊡ ⌂ | ⊗ Search ⊛ Favorites ⊛ Media ⊛ | ⊟• ⊜ ⊟ ⊟

Address ⊕ http://www.whales.org.au/discover/sperm/sperm2g.gif   ▼ ⬠ Go

2m

Done

This illustration on the **Discovering Whales: The Sperm Whale** page depicts the immense size of the sperm whale in comparison to an adult human being. More images and facts about this species and other cetaceans are offered by Whales on the Net, a Web site of Whales in Danger, an Australian conservation group.

the skin on the rest of a sperm whale's body has deep horizontal wrinkles. Other whales do not have this wrinkly look, and scientists are not sure why sperm whales do.

Sperm whales have relatively small flippers, and the dorsal fin on their backs is more of a bump than the kind of fin that you might see on a humpback whale, for example, or most dramatically on a killer whale.

Sperm whales have large mouths with very long and thin lower jaws. While most sperm whales are a dark brownish gray (unlike Moby Dick), their mouths are outlined in white and are white on the inside. Some scientists think the white mouths may become luminescent in deep water and then attract squid to the whales' open mouths.

▷ The Most Social Whales

As sperm whales dive, they hear the clicks of other sperm whales nearby. Except for the largest males, all whales seem to stay in groups. Whales in a group swim in rank, evenly spaced across the water, and they often dive at the same time. As they dive, they can hear the clicks of the other whales and know whether those whales have been successful in finding food.

Although whales are on the move most of the time, female and immature sperm whales stay in a specific area of the ocean. Usually this area is about 900 miles (1,450 kilometers) across.[13]

Female and young sperm whales live and move as members of "units," which seem to be like families, although all the whales in a unit may not be related to one another. A unit may consist of three whales or as many as twenty. Researchers believe that at least some members of the groups stay together for decades. Often the permanent units combine to form larger groups of twenty or thirty whales traveling together for days at a time.

In the 1800s, whalers noticed sperm whales' loyalty to others in the group. More recently, researchers have observed sperm whales swimming to help a companion being attacked by killer whales.

Strong Social Bonds

Scientists wonder about the basic groups or units formed by female and immature whales. What purpose do the groups serve that would make them such an important part of the whales' lives? One possibility is that sperm whales rely on their large size as defense against predators. When attacked by killer whales, sperm whales come together in a group, with the calves in the middle. If killer whales pull one group member away, another whale will swim to it and escort it back to the group.

Although sperm whales in a group usually dive for food at the same time and in rank, side by side, they probably hunt individually. Scientists are unable to watch sperm whales catch prey a thousand feet below the surface, but they have listened to them by using hydrophones, underwater microphones.

Group Formations

Being part of a group may help group members find food, though. Some scientists think the oldest

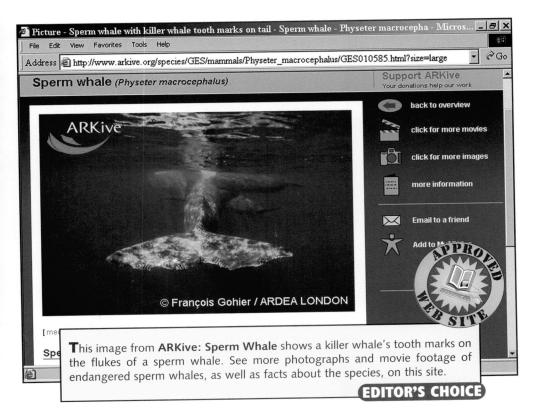

Picture - Sperm whale with killer whale tooth marks on tail - Sperm whale - Physeter macrocepha - Micros...

File   Edit   View   Favorites   Tools   Help

Address http://www.arkive.org/species/GES/mammals/Physeter_macrocephalus/GES010585.html?size=large   Go

Sperm whale *(Physeter macrocephalus)*

Support ARKive
Your donations help our work

back to overview

click for more movies

click for more images

more information

Email to a friend

Add to M...

© François Gohier / ARDEA LONDON

This image from **ARKive: Sperm Whale** shows a killer whale's tooth marks on the flukes of a sperm whale. See more photographs and movie footage of endangered sperm whales, as well as facts about the species, on this site.

EDITOR'S CHOICE

females may remember where the good hunting grounds are. Over time, whales may learn the habits of their prey and be able to anticipate changes in the ocean, such as in El Niño years. El Niños are flows of unusually warm surface waters that recur irregularly from east to west in the Pacific Ocean. This warmer-than-usual flow prevents the coldest water, rich in nutrients, from moving to the surface. It also disrupts weather patterns. Scientists think that experienced female whales might lead others in their unit to areas where plentiful food can be found under such conditions.

▲ *Sperm whales gathering in a group at the surface. Beneath the water's surface, they rub against each other to strengthen social bonds.*

Males also form groups, although the all-male groups are often smaller than the mixed groups of females and immature whales. Groups of males seem to become smaller as the males grow older, and the largest bull males may travel alone.

▷ Playtime

At least once a day, sperm whales in mixed groups of females and young whales gather at the surface for a few hours of rest, play, and communicating with one another. The whales seem to enjoy being close. Swimming just below the surface, whales may roll their bodies along the body of another whale or gently clasp jaws.

Resting whales look a little like logs floating on the water. But sometimes, they perform dramatic acrobatic stunts. One stunt is called a breach: A whale dives about three hundred feet (one hundred meters) down and then swims almost straight up, so that most of its body shoots up from the ocean's surface before it crashes into the water with a tremendous splash and loud noise.

Whales also seem to enjoy making noise by "lobtailing," lifting their back ends and huge flukes and then slamming them against the water. Lobtailing and breaching whales often perform the stunt several times in a row, and other whales may join in.

▶ Codas as Communication

During rest and playtime near the surface, the whales also communicate vocally. When sperm whales dive, they click loudly at regular intervals. When they gather near the surface, they click in patterns called codas, which sound a little like Morse code. For example, a coda might be "click, click, click, click, pause, click." Another might be "click, pause, click, click, click, click." Sometimes one whale will greet another whale with a partic- ular click pattern, and the other whale will answer with a different pattern. At other times, two whales click the same pattern at almost the same time.

The first scientific report of whale codas was in 1977.[14] Since then, researchers have listened for this unusual form of communication and have collected recordings. As with many details of sperm whale behavior, codas are still a mystery.

Evidence suggests that codas are a form of communication, but biologists can only guess what information is being passed from one whale to another. Codas seem to be something that whales learn, because whales that live near the island nation of Sri Lanka, in the Indian Ocean, use different click patterns than the whales living near the Galápagos Islands, in the Pacific, many miles away. One researcher noticed that when whales communicate with codas, other whales at a distance become silent. His assumption is that the whales pay attention when they hear codas.[15]

▶ Intelligence

Some sperm whale behavior suggests that the whales learn from one another, and that ability to learn may indicate what we understand as intelligence. Scientists do not yet fully understand intelligence in humans. They are still making discoveries about the human brain and how it works. So it is easy to see how much more difficult it is

▽ A close-up of the back of a sperm whale. The black hole to the left front of its body is its blowhole.

to understand intelligence in a species so different from humans. Still, evidence that whales from different groups "speak" different codas suggests that the codas are a learned form of communication, part of whale culture. The complex social lives of whales also suggest a whale culture.

One reason to wonder about the intelligence of sperm whales is that they have the largest brain of any mammal on Earth. Of course, the rest of a sperm whale is also large, although some other whales, including blue whales and fin whales, are larger. Analysis of sperm whale brains has shown that the part of the brain that "thinks" and might be partly responsible for personality is large and well developed in sperm whale brains. The part that probably controls emotions is not well developed.[16]

Raising Calves

One possible reason for the tightly knit units of female sperm whales might be that caring for very young whales, known as calves, seems to require the cooperation of several adults.

Sperm whales have the lowest reproductive rate of any mammal. Adult females give birth once every four to twenty years, and when they do, it is only to one calf at a time, after a gestation of about sixteen months. The calf is dependent on its mother's milk for several years.

Although newborn calves weigh approximately one ton (907 kilograms) and measure 11 to 16

▲ Sperm whales rarely jump fully out of the water when they come up for air. From this photo, one might even mistake a sperm whale for a submarine.

feet (3.4 to 4.9 meters) from nose to flukes, they are vulnerable to predators such as sharks and killer whales. The calves cannot stay close to their mothers all the time because they cannot manage the deep dives.

A young calf swims along the water's surface, staying above its mother by listening to her clicks. However, a mother who is so far below the surface might not be able to protect her calf at the surface. Observers have noticed that other whales in the group often escort young calves as they swim above their mothers. Instead of diving at the same time, whales in the group stagger their dives so that at least one whale is at the surface more of the time.

One marine biologist who was fortunate enough to see a sperm whale being born noted that other females quickly crowded around the calf, making physical contact with it.[17] Some evidence suggests that females in addition to the mother produce milk for the calf.

▶ Growing Up

If the calf is a female, she may stay with the group the rest of her life. Males leave the females when they are about six years old. These young males usually find other young males and form bachelor groups, although the bachelor groups are usually smaller than the groups of adult females and immature whales.

Life is very different for males after they leave the mixed groups. They spend more time in colder waters, closer to the North and South Poles. Their

▼ This calf swims very close to its mother and a pod of other sperm whales in this photo taken near the coast of Guam.

diet changes as they eat more fish than squid, and they may eat larger squid. They will probably not have any contact with mixed groups again until they are close to thirty years old. During their years apart from mixed groups, the young males grow—a lot.

▶ Breeding Males

About twenty years after leaving the mixed group, male sperm whales might head to warmer waters in search of females to breed and father calves. By this time, the male is much larger than a female and may weigh three times as much.

When a male finds a group of female whales, he makes a loud clang to announce his presence.

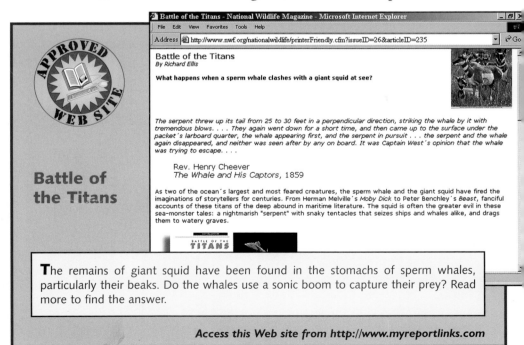

Battle of the Titans

Battle of the Titans - National Wildlife Magazine - Microsoft Internet Explorer

File   Edit   View   Favorites   Tools   Help

Address   http://www.nwf.org/nationalwildlife/printerFriendly.cfm?issueID=26&articleID=235   Go

Battle of the Titans
By Richard Ellis

What happens when a sperm whale clashes with a giant squid at see?

The serpent threw up its tail from 25 to 30 feet in a perpendicular direction, striking the whale by it with tremendous blows. . . . They again went down for a short time, and then came up to the surface under the packet's larboard quarter, the whale appearing first, and the serpent in pursuit . . . the serpent and the whale again disappeared, and neither was seen after by any on board. It was Captain West's opinion that the whale was trying to escape. . . .

Rev. Henry Cheever
The Whale and His Captors, 1859

As two of the ocean's largest and most feared creatures, the sperm whale and the giant squid have fired the imaginations of storytellers for centuries. From Herman Melville's *Moby Dick* to Peter Benchley's *Beast*, fanciful accounts of these titans of the deep abound in maritime literature. The squid is often the greater evil in these sea-monster tales: a nightmarish "serpent" with snaky tentacles that seizes ships and whales alike, and drags them to watery graves.

TITANS

The remains of giant squid have been found in the stomachs of sperm whales, particularly their beaks. Do the whales use a sonic boom to capture their prey? Read more to find the answer.

Access this Web site from http://www.myreportlinks.com

As one biologist observed, all members of the group seem delighted to be in the presence of the enormous male. Females and immature males crowd around the adult who is so much larger than they are and roll against his body. The male may spend several hours with the group before swimming off to find another group.[18]

Only the largest males join female groups to breed, and even these large bull whales do not seem to breed every year. Researchers have not seen the breeding males act aggressively toward one another in the breeding ground. Instead, the bull whales seem to avoid one another. Still, biologists have seen long white scars on the heads of these males, and they believe the scars were caused by the teeth of other large whales during fights. The fact that bull whales grow to be so large indicates that size and strength matter as they compete for females.

Scientists are not certain about the average life span of sperm whales, but the whales seem to live a long time, perhaps as long as seventy years. So many of the largest and oldest sperm whales were killed by whaling in the 1900s that sperm whale populations today probably do not look much like those that swam the seas before whaling devastated their numbers.

Chapter 3

DANGERS OF THE DEEP

In the past, whaling reduced the sperm whale population to perhaps one third of its pre-whaling numbers. The population is recovering, but slowly, partly because sperm whales reproduce so slowly, as all top predators in a food chain do. Another reason for the slow recovery may be that whalers often killed the largest, most mature whales that were so important to producing future generations.

▶ Yankee Whaling

After discovering the existence of sperm whales in the early 1700s, Yankee whalers quickly turned their attention to hunting them. Shipbuilders built larger ships so the whalers could venture farther into the ocean, but the whalers of the early 1700s still needed to stay close to land. Whale blubber does not keep well; as it begins to spoil, it produces oil of a much lower quality. When whalers killed a sperm whale, they had to tow the dead whale to land to cook the blubber.

By 1815 the whaling ships like those described in the novel *Moby Dick* were in general use. These wooden ships had three masts with square sails. They were about one hundred feet (thirty meters) long and could carry about three hundred tons (two hundred seventy metric tons). Hanging from the ship were the whaleboats in which crews of six men rowed close to their enormous prey. Planks extended from one side of the ship so men could stand above a dead whale strapped to the side of the ship and cut it up.

An important innovation in the whaling ship of that time was the brick oven containing large iron kettles, called tryworks, that enabled the whalers to render, or melt down, the whale blubber into

▽ *A small boat of men attacking a right whale with spears. The painting is believed to date between 1856 and 1907.*

its oil and store it in barrels immediately. The onboard oven meant that whaling ship crews did not need to rush to land to render whales they caught.[1] Whaling ships left port intending to stay at sea for years.

The Hunt

Whaling was dangerous work. Even the man standing lookout high on the ship's mast was hardly safe. One sailor at a time would stand for two hours on boards nailed to the mast, about one hundred feet (thirty meters) above the deck, with two iron hoops to keep him from falling.[2] As he scanned the ocean for a whale's spout, he would need to be able to tell from miles away whether or not it was a sperm whale spout or the exhaled breath of a fin whale or gray whale. (Compared to other whales, sperm whales exhale a low, bushy spout.)

When whalers found whales, the ship's crew sprang to action. Men lowered whaleboats and raced each other toward the whales. The whaleboats were about thirty feet (nine meters) long and six feet (two meters) wide and pointed at each

▼ *Two whales blowing at the ocean's surface.*

end. Each whaleboat held six men, including the harpooner, a "boatheader," who steered the boat, and four men to row.[3]

As the thirty-foot (nine-meter) boat neared the whale—which, if it was a male, might be almost twice as long as the boat—the harpooner stood to throw the harpoon. The harpoon was not meant to kill the whale, but rather to attach the boat to the whale. A nine-hundred-foot- (two hundred seventy-meter-) long rope was attached to the harpoon.

▶ The Kill

When the harpoon pierced the whale and the wounded whale thrashed in pain, the crew of the small boat rowed away as fast as they could to avoid being smashed. Then the whale usually dove. When it surfaced again, it usually swam, dragging the whaleboat with it. The men in the whaleboat could only hope that the whale would not drag them so far from the ship that it would not be able to find them.

Finally, as the whale became exhausted, the crew could bring the whaleboat close again. The harpooner and the boatheader then very carefully changed places so the boatheader could kill the whale by thrusting long lances, or spears, into the whale's heart or lungs.[4] After hours of strenuous work, the whaleboat crew towed the dead whale back to the ship.

Not all chases were successful. Sometimes the crew would row for hours without even getting close enough to harpoon the whale. Other times, whaleboats were overturned by the whale or by a storm. One important piece of equipment on every whaleboat was a hatchet used to cut the line that attached the boat to the whale if the whale dove deep or swam too far.

▲ Four crewmen mince, or cut up, the blubber of a caught sperm whale. This photo was taken in 1903 aboard the sailing ship California, off the coast of Japan.

Cutting Up the Whale

As soon as the whale could be brought to the ship and fastened to its side, the crew set to work, racing the sharks to claim all they could from the whale. They cut away the blubber and cut it into pieces small enough for the tryworks kettles. The oil was then stored in barrels.

The crew used buckets to scoop oil from the spermaceti organ. The spermaceti oil was worth three to five times as much as any other whale oil, so it was stored separately. A large male might carry as much as 500 gallons (1,893 liters) of the precious liquid wax.[5] Oil from the "junk" just below the spermaceti organ was not as valuable as the spermaceti oil, but still was more valuable than other whale oil.

New Whaling Methods

In the late 1860s, a Norwegian named Svend Foyn invented the harpoon cannon, which propelled the harpoon much farther than the arm of a harpooner could. Soon the harpoons themselves were designed to explode inside the whale to kill it.

The steamboat was invented in the same decade. The harpoon cannon coupled with steam-powered boats made it possible for whalers to kill whales that were too fast for the wooden whaling boats and hand-thrown harpoons. The fast rorquals, which include blue and fin whales, had escaped the early nineteenth-century whalers, but the harpoon cannon and steam-powered boats allowed whalers to slaughter them. By the end of the nineteenth century, hundreds of thousands had been killed.

In 1925 the first factory ship with a stern slipway appeared. The stern slipway was a huge chute that took the whale to modern factory works inside the ship. Norway became the leader among whaling countries, and later Japan and the Soviet Union took the lead.

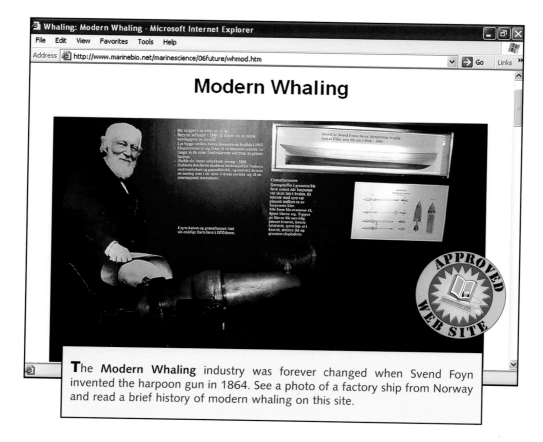

The **Modern Whaling** industry was forever changed when Svend Foyn invented the harpoon gun in 1864. See a photo of a factory ship from Norway and read a brief history of modern whaling on this site.

▶ Sperm Whales Are Hunted Again

As whalers chased the huge blue and fin whales, sperm whales lived in relative peace. That ended in the late 1940s when whalers had killed so many of the large rorqual whales that these whales had almost disappeared. In addition, people had found new markets for the spermaceti oil. The oil made a superior lubricant, which was used in automatic transmissions in cars and for delicate high-altitude equipment. It was also used in other products, including vitamins and detergents.

The record catch of sperm whales was 29,255 in 1964.[6] A Japanese expert on sperm whales estimated that 261,505 sperm whales were killed just in the North Pacific between 1910 and 1966.[7]

▶ The End of Whaling—Almost

In 1982 the International Whaling Commission declared a moratorium on commercial whaling, which meant commercial whaling was supposed to stop. The moratorium does allow exceptions, and Japanese whalers still hunt sperm whales for "scientific research." More threatening to whales than scientific research is the possibility that the moratorium may end. Several countries would like to resume commercial whaling. In fact, Norway has decided to ignore the moratorium and hunt minke whales, and Iceland is again hunting whales.

The Effects of Whaling

Sperm whale expert Hal Whitehead has estimated that a population of more than a million sperm whales in the early eighteenth century has been reduced to about 360,000 animals, about one third of what it was. But Whitehead believes that the harm to the sperm whale population is more than a matter of numbers. The huge breeding males almost disappeared.

The biologist noted that the number of large males among sperm whales killed off the coast of Peru fell from 35 percent between 1958 and 1961 to 2 percent between 1979 and 1981. In 1981, only one of the 225 sperm whales killed was a large male.[8]

APPROVED WEB SITE

Eight European States Hit With Legal Action Over Whale Protection

Eight European States Hit With Legal Action Over Whale Protection - Microsoft Internet Explorer

File   Edit   View   Favorites   Tools   Help

Address   http://www.ens-newswire.com/ens/dec2005/2005-12-20-04.asp   Go

Power your laptop from the sun...

Guaranteed!
www.ctsolar.com

THE OCEAN FOUNDATION
202.887.8992
www.oceanfdn.org

Eight European States Hit With Legal Action Over Whale Protection

BRUSSELS, Belgium, December 20, 2005 (ENS) - Protective measures taken to ensure the health and survival of whales, dolphins and porpoises in European waters are not being adequately monitored by eight European Union countries, the European Commission says. To achieve better monitoring, the Commission today launched legal proceedings against the eight governments.

All cetacean species require strict protection under the EU's Habitats directive, or law. The Commission considers that Belgium, France, Greece, Italy, the Netherlands, Portugal, Spain and the UK have not established effective surveillance systems to monitor that protection.

The Commission has taken first step in the legal procedure by sending these member states a first written warning that they are

Ads by Google

EU Directive information
& legislative materials relating to EU financial services & company law
www.complinet.com

Whale Watching Costa Rica
Humpbacks, pseudo orcas, dolphins & rainforest in beautiful Drake Bay
www.drakebay.info

Dolphin & whale watching
Year round intimate Dolphin & Whale Safaris on hi-tech

This *Environment News Service* story reports that the European Commission has launched legal proceedings against eight European Union countries for not adequately monitoring the whales, dolphins, and porpoises in their waters.

Access this Web site from http://www.myreportlinks.com

The sperm whale population also lost many mature females. These females may have been the ones that knew the best places to find food, especially when climate and ocean current conditions changed, as during an El Niño year. Mature females may also have kept groups together.

Whitehead noted that when he studied sperm whales off the coast of the Galápagos Islands in 1995, he and his crew saw no small calves.[9] Unless new sperm whales are born to replace those that die, the population will continue to shrink. The sperm whales' slow rate of reproduction is considered one of the major threats to the species' survival.[10]

▷ Pollution

The threat of whaling still looms on the horizon, but sperm whales and other ocean inhabitants also face other threats. One very serious problem is pollution.

Until a few decades ago, people believed that the ocean was big enough to absorb all the waste they cared to dump in it. People disposed of radioactive waste and chemical weapons, as well as garbage, in the ocean and thought they were doing no harm. Finally, in 1972, countries around the world signed the London Convention, an international treaty that limits the waste material that can be disposed of at sea. Amendments have since

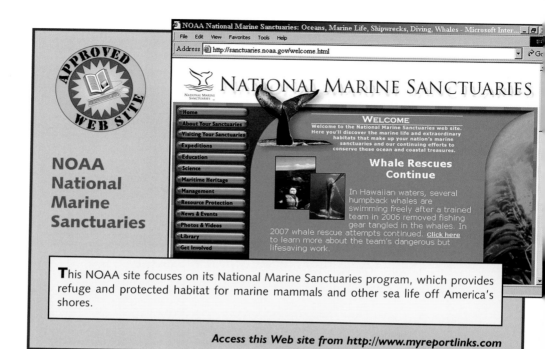

NOAA National Marine Sanctuaries

NOAA National Marine Sanctuaries: Oceans, Marine Life, Shipwrecks, Diving, Whales - Microsoft Inter...

File   Edit   View   Favorites   Tools   Help

Address http://sanctuaries.noaa.gov/welcome.html

NATIONAL MARINE SANCTUARIES

- Home
- About Your Sanctuaries
- Visiting Your Sanctuaries
- Expeditions
- Education
- Science
- Maritime Heritage
- Management
- Resource Protection
- News & Events
- Photos & Videos
- Library
- Get Involved

WELCOME

Welcome to the National Marine Sanctuaries web site. Here you'll discover the marine life and extraordinary habitats that make up your nation's marine sanctuaries and our continuing efforts to conserve these ocean and coastal treasures.

Whale Rescues Continue

In Hawaiian waters, several humpback whales are swimming freely after a trained team in 2006 removed fishing gear tangled in the whales. In 2007 whale rescue attempts continued. Click here to learn more about the team's dangerous but lifesaving work.

This NOAA site focuses on its National Marine Sanctuaries program, which provides refuge and protected habitat for marine mammals and other sea life off America's shores.

Access this Web site from http://www.myreportlinks.com

added new materials to the list of things that cannot be dumped into the oceans.

By the 1990s, ocean dumping had been reduced to a fraction of what it was in the 1970s. But that fraction still adds up to millions of tons of industrial waste added to what was dumped in the past. Most of the waste dumped in the 1990s came from Japan and the Republic of Korea.[11] Partly due to the restrictions imposed by the London Convention, many countries found other ways to dispose of industrial waste. Recycling and cleaner production technologies have also helped reduce waste.

▶ Where Pollution Comes From

Many dangerous chemicals, as well as familiar garbage such as plastic bags, still enter the ocean through drains and rivers. For example, fertilizers and pesticides seep into rivers that carry the chemicals to the ocean. Chemicals used on farms and in industry, along with garbage, account for about 44 percent of ocean pollution. Another 33 percent comes from pollution in the atmosphere.[12]

Many of the chemicals that now end up in the ocean did not even exist fifty years ago. New chemicals are developed to manufacture everything from computers to toys. The exact names of these synthetic chemicals are often long and difficult to remember, but they are slowly changing our environment.

▶ Why Pollution Threatens Whales

In the ocean, tiny creatures such as plankton absorb polluting chemicals. These chemicals can build up in the smaller animals and fish, becoming more concentrated. When larger fish eat the smaller ones, they absorb the concentrated chemicals. Animals at the top of the food chain, such as sperm whales, take in the highest levels of concentrated chemicals. (Baleen whales are often lower in a food chain.) Partly because of their thick layers of blubber, whales store the pollutants in their bodies.

The polluting chemicals can affect whales in various ways. Scientists are especially concerned about the harm such chemicals do to animals' immune systems, which control their ability to fight disease. They are also worried about what those chemicals are doing to the whales' ability to reproduce.

For some time, scientists have been studying the harmful effects of heavy metals such as mercury. Mercury does not break down in the environment. In fact, it converts to molecules that can be digested and accumulate in the body. Tests have shown that mercury is a nerve toxin particularly harmful to the brain.

▲ These are not clouds traveling across the water's surface. They are angled sprays from the blowholes of two sperm whales barely visible in the photo. This type of spray is unique to the sperm whale and a primary way of distinguishing it from a distance.

We might expect the oceans near the North and South Poles to be much cleaner, with less pollution because they are far from industry. However, scientists have learned that air and water currents bring polluting chemicals from all over the world to these oceans. The chemicals then settle in the cold water where they take longer to break down because the water is so cold.[13] These are the oceans where male sperm whales spend most of their lives.

The oceans are also absorbing airborne carbon dioxide from industry and automobile emissions. The carbon dioxide is changing the pH balance in the ocean and causing it to be more acidic.

Noise Pollution

Another form of pollution is noise. The oceans have become much noisier during the past century. Not only are more ships and larger ships churning across the oceans, but people are purposefully making noise deep in the ocean.

For example, as oil companies look for oil under the ocean, they fire large air guns to make seismic (earthquake-like) pulses. They use the sound to learn about rock layers beneath the ocean—in much the same way that sperm whales use loud sounds to find their food.

Ocean sounds also include the Low-Frequency Active (LFA) sonar the U.S. Navy has been testing to detect the presence of enemy submarines. The system includes underwater transmitters that send very loud "pings," which can travel hundreds of miles through the water.

Noise pollution may be affecting whales in several ways. One effect may be hearing loss due to exposure to sudden intense noise or continued exposure to noise. Sperm whales depend on their hearing to find food. Two sperm whales killed when a ship ran into them were found to have ear damage.[14]

Noise pollution may also mask the sounds that whales listen for. As biologists have observed sperm whales in noisy situations, they have noticed

A whaling ship is anchored in the distance as its crew in small boats harpoon sperm whales in this painting from 1825.

that the whales seem to make fewer of the creaks that probably mean they are closing in on prey.

Ship Strikes

Large, fast ships sometimes run into whales that do not get out of the way fast enough. Other whale species, especially fin whales and right whales, are killed more often by large ships. However, sperm whales are killed by ships each year, and the number will most likely increase as more and faster ships speed across the ocean.

Drift Nets

Fishing gear presents another danger. In the past, many fishermen used drift nets to catch fish in the ocean. These nets can be miles long and made of synthetic material that lasts a very long time. In 1991 the United Nations (UN) passed a resolution banning the use of drift nets on the high seas, but drift nets abandoned years ago still float in the ocean. Seabirds, dolphins, and whales can get tangled in the drift nets and drown.

Illegal drift nets are the main cause of sperm whale deaths in the Mediterranean Sea, according to a 2004 report to the International Union for the Conservation of Nature.[15] The whales do have a friend in the area, though. A biologist named Dr. Antonio Di Natale leads a rescue team to help whales trapped in nets. The team cuts away as much of the netting as possible working from boats. Then divers, including Di Natale himself, go into the water close to trapped whales to cut away any remaining net.

Di Natale remembers one whale—a huge male—in particular. The team had succeeded in cutting away only some of the net before losing the whale in rough seas. A week later the rescuers found him again. The whale was very stressed with net around his head and in his mouth. The whale let Di Natale put his hands inside its mouth, but removing the net was painful. Suddenly the

This female sperm whale fought so forcefully to free herself from a synthetic line that the struggle broke her jaw. The resulting infection killed her and her unborn offspring. At the Web site of **Cetacean Society International**, access a photo gallery, current news issues, action alerts, and more.

whale's clicks changed to such a loud clang that the biologist had to retreat.

As the whale began to click again, the biologist returned and again the whale let him reach inside its mouth. When the whale was finally free, he seemed grateful—rather than swimming away, he stayed close to the boat for two hours.[16]

In some areas, fishermen using long lines to catch fish have observed male sperm whales taking fish from the fishing lines. One biologist noted reports that angry fishermen sometimes shoot whales.[17]

The number of sperm whales killed by ships and fishing gear each year is small compared to the total sperm whale population. At the same time, sperm whales reproduce more slowly than any other mammal. As the ocean becomes more dangerous, sperm whales may be killed faster than the species can reproduce.

▶ Global Warming

Another threat that scientists are just beginning to understand is global warming. Scientists believe that melting ice at the North and South Poles is changing the climate in the ocean. How these changes might affect sperm whales is not clear.

Scientists have already observed that the temperature of the oceans is changing. The oceans are getting warmer. As the temperature changes, currents also change. Fish that have adapted to certain temperatures are now found where they were never seen before. Some species of fish and smaller organisms that require cold temperatures may disappear.

As currents and ocean temperatures change, so will the location of whales' food. If whales rely on memory to find food, they will find that their knowledge is no longer useful.

Killer Whales

Sperm whales do have a natural enemy in the ocean. Killer whales, although much smaller than sperm whales, occasionally attack sperm whales and can kill them.

Observers have been surprised by how passively sperm whales react to attacks by killer whales. The sperm whales gather in a formation called a marguerite, with all of their heads toward the center and their flukes outward. Calves are kept in the center of the formation.

▼ Saving a whale that has become stranded is far from easy. Even if a whale is kept wet and fed constantly, if it is not kept upright, its lungs can collapse under its own weight.

Strandings

Occasionally, whales seem to die by propelling themselves onto beaches. This behavior is called stranding. Stranded whales are often sick, old, or wounded. Wounded whales may show evidence of having been caught in fishnets.

Sometimes all the whales in a group of sperm whales strand together. Disease may cause a group of whales or dolphins to strand together. In other cases, biologists examining stranded whales have found that they were healthy before they stranded. Because sperm whales have such strong social bonds, all the whales in a group may follow a sick whale onto land. Some scientists think a leader in the group may simply make a navigational error and lead the group onto land. One theory is that earthquakes or testing of Navy sonar may chase whales onto the shore. Not all whale species mass strand, however. Baleen whales do not strand as a group.

Individuals involved in trying to save stranded whales have a difficult time, as one might imagine. First, the animals need to be kept wet and cooled, with water poured over them to keep them hydrated. Second, they need to be sent back into the ocean, and this is often not easily done. Finally, even when some whales swim back to sea, they turn around and strand again, for reasons scientists still do not understand.

PROTECTION FOR WHALES

Today, efforts to save whales come from many directions. Governments, international organizations, and conservation organizations are looking for ways to help whales survive.

▷ The International Whaling Commission: Early Years

The future of whales was the topic of discussion for representatives of fifteen countries that met in 1946. These individuals were concerned that some species of whales seemed to be disappearing. However, they were concerned not about the welfare of the whales themselves but about the welfare of the whaling industry.

Realizing that the industry was killing off entire species of whales, they drafted the International Convention for the Regulation of Whaling to preserve whale stocks, or populations, as a resource for people. They agreed whaling needed to be regulated to prevent economic hardship of whaling countries.[1] The International Whaling Commission was created to enforce

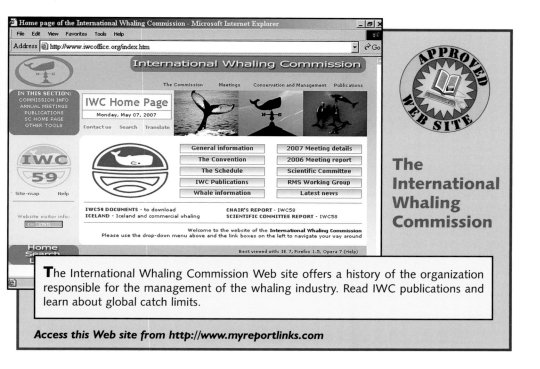

The International Whaling Commission Web site offers a history of the organization responsible for the management of the whaling industry. Read IWC publications and learn about global catch limits.

Access this Web site from http://www.myreportlinks.com

the International Convention for the Regulation of Whaling.

▷ Failure of Quotas

However, the IWC failed to protect whale stocks. The basis of the convention was that member countries would work together in their own interest to protect the industry. A scientific committee gathered information about whale populations, and member countries were supposed to set quotas, or shares of the total, based on scientific information.

In fact, countries ignored the IWC's scientific findings and continued to kill so many whales that several species, such as the blue whale, came close to becoming extinct. The IWC countries put greed before protection of whale species.

The IWC does not have the ability to enforce its own rules. Any country that disagrees with a quota can simply say that it will not abide by the decision. The former Soviet Union, a leading whaling nation in the twentieth century, chose to ignore IWC quotas and then not accurately report how many whales it killed. From 1948 to 1973, the Soviet Union killed more than 48,000 humpback whales but told the IWC that it had killed only 2,710.[2]

Changing Attitudes

During the 1960s the focus of the IWC began to change. The whales were disappearing; the business of whaling offered less profit. In addition, several biologists began to listen to the songs of humpback whales, and they wrote about these wonderful animals. People began to pay attention to whales.

In general, people were becoming more aware of the environment and species in danger of becoming extinct. As early as 1948, conservationists from around the world came together to form the International Union for the Protection of Nature. The organization, now known as the IUCN-World Conservation Union, is still active today, promoting awareness of the environment.

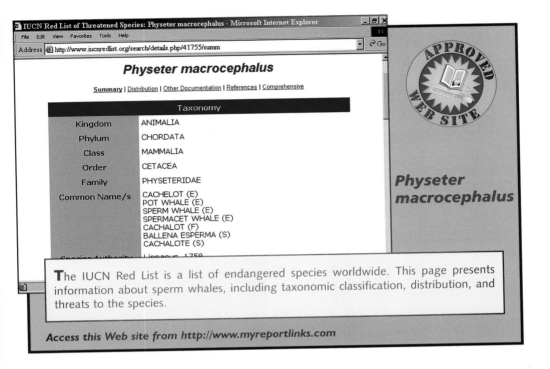

Physeter macrocephalus

The IUCN Red List is a list of endangered species worldwide. This page presents information about sperm whales, including taxonomic classification, distribution, and threats to the species.

Access this Web site from http://www.myreportlinks.com

The IUCN developed criteria to measure the well-being of a species and determine if that species is threatened or endangered. Using these criteria, the IUCN publishes a "red list" of endangered species. The IUCN also developed an international treaty known as CITES: The Convention on International Trade in Endangered Species of Wild Fauna and Flora. This treaty is intended to ensure that international trade in wild animals and plants does not threaten their survival.

▷ Legal Protection in the United States

In the early 1970s the United States Congress passed two bills designed to protect endangered species. The Marine Mammal Protection Act, which became law in 1972, makes it illegal for anyone to kill or harm any marine mammal, including whales. The Endangered Species Act of 1973 makes it illegal to kill or harm a member of an endangered species.

The Endangered Species Act also provides for steps to be taken to help endangered species thrive. It requires that the Department of the Interior bring

▼ *The head of a sperm whale is almost one third the size of its total body length. Notice the typical indentations and wrinkles on this whale's body.*

together experts to develop recovery plans for species in danger of extinction. In 2006 the National Oceanic and Atmospheric Administration (NOAA) completed a draft Sperm Whale Recovery Plan. One goal of the recovery plan is obtaining a better estimate of just how many sperm whales there are and whether or not the number is increasing. Another goal is identifying and pro-tecting important habitat.[3]

Laws passed in the United States might seem to provide little protection for animals that spend most of their time many miles from any country. But the United States—which led the world in whaling during the 1800s—took the belief that whales needed protection to the International Whaling Commission. Other countries with the same attitude joined the IWC during the 1970s. By the end of the decade, antiwhaling members were in the majority.[4]

▷ United Nations (UN) Convention on the Law of the Sea

The 1970s brought another important development in protection for whales. In 1973, representatives from many countries came together for the Third United Nations Conference on the Law of the Sea.

The idea of laws governing the oceans was a new one. For centuries, countries had followed a freedom-of-the-seas doctrine. The oceans were free for all and belonged to no one. During the 1900s, though, freedom of the seas led to conflict among countries. Areas of conflict included ocean pollution and the question of who might claim resources under the ocean.

The UN conference that met first in 1973 worked out an international treaty—called the United Nations Convention on the Law of the Sea (UNCLOS)—which was adopted in 1982.[5] Two parts of UNCLOS proved to be important for whales. First, the treaty provides for a 200-mile (322-kilometer) exclusive economic zone extending from a country's coastline. Countries have the right to control the fish and animals within that zone. Because of UNCLOS, the United States' protection of whales extends 200 miles (322 kilometers) into the Atlantic and Pacific Oceans. In addition, UNCLOS states specifically that all countries signing the treaty are obligated to conserve marine mammals, especially whales.[6]

▷ The IWC Moratorium

In 1982 the IWC voted for a moratorium on whaling. The moratorium reduced all whaling quotas to zero for the next five years. The moratorium was later extended indefinitely.

The IWC moratorium does not forbid all whaling. One exception is allowed for subsistence whaling by indigenous people for their own use. For such people, whaling provides meat and other materials that are considered necessary for their way of life. Examples of indigenous people include the Inuit of Alaska, who are allowed to kill bowhead whales, and native people of Greenland. This exception is only granted to people who have a long cultural tradition of killing whales for their own needs.

The IWC also provided a scientific research exception to the moratorium. The scientific research exception allows any country to decide

▽ *Inuits launch a whaleboat off Prince of Wales, the second largest island in Alaska, as seen in this photo from 1929. Whaling has been a part of Inuit culture for thousands of years.*

how many whales it should kill for scientific research. Japan has taken advantage of this loophole to kill sperm whales, minke whales, and Bryde's whales. In 2005, Japan killed more than seven hundred whales by claiming those kills were scientifically necessary.[7]

▶ A New Role for IWC

The IWC changed its emphasis from setting quotas for killing whales to looking for ways to protect them. From its beginning, the IWC has had three parts. The scientific committee analyzes information about whales and then makes recommendations to the technical committee. The technical committee puts the findings of the scientific committee into proposed amendments to be considered at annual meetings of the IWC. The finance and administration committee manages the IWC.

During the past five decades, the scientific committee has grown from eleven scientists in 1954 to more than 170 participants in 2003. These days the scientific committee studies environmental concerns, methods of identifying whales to count them, and whale watching.

The IWC has set boundaries for whale sanctuaries, beginning with the Indian Ocean Sanctuary, established in 1979. Parts of the Pacific Ocean off the coast of Mexico and most of the oceans in the Southern Hemisphere have also been designated as whale sanctuaries. In 1994 the IWC designated the Southern Ocean Sanctuary. In 2004 it confirmed an Antarctic sanctuary defined by France ten years earlier.

IWC Politics

Since the 1970s, when antiwhaling countries joined the IWC to protest whaling, the pro- and antiwhaling countries have accused each other of unfair political tactics. Japan is reported to have given fishing aid that equals $100 million U.S. dollars to Pacific and Caribbean countries that voted with Japan.[8]

Japan has denied using its aid to pressure countries to vote with it and has, in turn, accused antiwhaling countries including the United States, Australia, and the United Kingdom of buying votes on a larger scale than Japan could by itself.

In fact, the United States is very influential in the IWC. Because the IWC has no way to enforce its rules and decisions, it relies on economic sanctions to convince countries to abide by its rules. Several times during the 1970s, the United States threatened to ban the import of fishing products from countries that did not stay within IWC quotas. The threats proved enough to convince the countries to limit whaling.

For example, the American Cetacean Society took its opposition to the Japan Whaling

Association to the Supreme Court of the United States in the 1980s. The purpose of the lawsuit was to pressure the U.S. secretary of commerce to use economic sanctions to encourage Japan to abide by the IWC moratorium. Although the Court ruled that sanctions were not required, the case resulted in negotiations with Japan, and Japan agreed to abide by the moratorium's restrictions.[9]

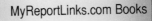

THE WORK OF RESEARCHERS

Despite the fact that whalers have killed hundreds of thousands of sperm whales and cut them apart, scientists have a surprising number of unanswered questions about these huge, shy animals. One reason we know so little about sperm whales is that they spend so much of their time deep in the ocean. They are difficult to find and to observe.

At the same time, any hopes of helping sperm whales recover from the losses of whaling depend on researchers knowing what the whales need in order to thrive. In recent decades, governments, universities, and conservation organizations have invested in research to benefit whales.

▶ Questions

To save the species from extinction, scientists need to know how many sperm whales there are and how fast they are reproducing. Has the loss of so many mature males to whaling resulted in fewer

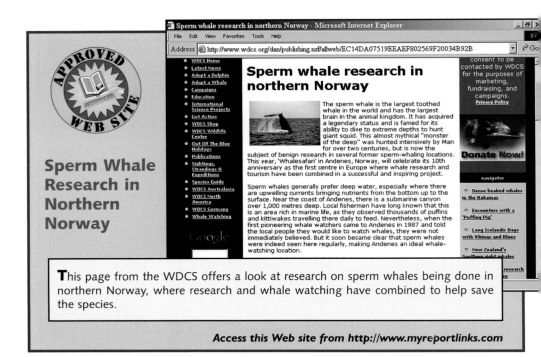

Sperm Whale Research in Northern Norway

Sperm whale research in northern Norway

The sperm whale is the largest toothed whale in the world and has the largest brain in the animal kingdom. It has acquired a legendary status and is famed for its ability to dive to extreme depths to hunt giant squid. This almost mythical "monster of the deep" was hunted intensively by Man for over two centuries, but is now the subject of benign research in several former sperm-whaling locations. This year, 'Whalesafari' in Andenes, Norway, will celebrate its 10th anniversary as the first centre in Europe where whale research and tourism have been combined in a successful and inspiring project.

Sperm whales generally prefer deep water, especially where there are upwelling currents bringing nutrients from the bottom up to the surface. Near the coast of Andenes, there is a submarine canyon over 1,000 metres deep. Local fishermen have long known that this is an area rich in marine life, as they observed thousands of puffins and kittiwakes travelling there daily to feed. Nevertheless, when the first pioneering whale watchers came to Andenes in 1987 and told the local people they would like to watch whales, they were not immediately believed. But it soon became clear that sperm whales were indeed seen here regularly, making Andenes an ideal whale-watching location.

This page from the WDCS offers a look at research on sperm whales being done in northern Norway, where research and whale watching have combined to help save the species.

Access this Web site from http://www.myreportlinks.com

calves in recent years? Are social groups necessary for raising calves, and has the death of mature females during whaling years caused social groups to break up?

Scientists also need to understand what the whales need from their habitat and what factors are having an impact on them. Will whales be able to adjust to rapid changes in their environment caused by pollution, increased shipping, and global warming? Is pollution killing whales? Is it interfering with their ability to reproduce? Is increased noise in the ocean making it difficult for whales to find food and communicate with each other? These are all critical questions.

▷ Research by Whalers

Some of what scientists know about sperm whales comes from research done on whaling ships. When whalers pursued sperm whales in the 1900s, they often took scientists with them. The whalers wanted to know more about sperm whales so they could find them and kill them more efficiently. They also hoped to manage whaling so the whales would be a sustainable resource. In other words, they hoped to be able to kill whales without destroying the population altogether.

As the scientists on whaling ships examined dead sperm whales, they began to learn about sperm whales' lives. When they examined the dead whales' skin, they found different parasites on males and females traveling together and concluded that males do not stay with females. The whales' teeth helped scientists estimate age. Examining what was in the whales' stomachs helped scientists understand what they ate.[1]

Whalers also shot metal tags labeled with serial numbers into whales that they did not kill at the time. When the tagged whales were eventually killed, scientists could see how far the whale had traveled during the time the tag was in it. For example, a tag was shot into a male off the coast of Nova Scotia. Seven years later the male was killed off the coast of Spain, on the other side of the Atlantic Ocean.[2]

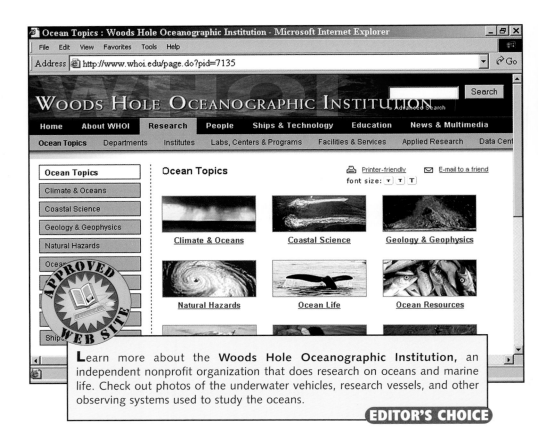

Ocean Topics : Woods Hole Oceanographic Institution - Microsoft Internet Explorer

File   Edit   View   Favorites   Tools   Help

Address   http://www.whoi.edu/page.do?pid=7135   Go

WOODS HOLE OCEANOGRAPHIC INSTITUTION   Search

Home   About WHOI   **Research**   People   Ships & Technology   Education   News & Multimedia

Ocean Topics   Departments   Institutes   Labs, Centers & Programs   Facilities & Services   Applied Research   Data Cent

Ocean Topics   **Ocean Topics**   Printer-friendly   E-mail to a friend

Climate & Oceans   font size: T T T

Coastal Science

Geology & Geophysics

Natural Hazards   Climate & Oceans   Coastal Science   Geology & Geophysics

Ocea

Natural Hazards   Ocean Life   Ocean Resources

Ship

Learn more about the **Woods Hole Oceanographic Institution,** an independent nonprofit organization that does research on oceans and marine life. Check out photos of the underwater vehicles, research vessels, and other observing systems used to study the oceans.

EDITOR'S CHOICE

▶ Listening to Whales

Early research also includes the work of a zoologist at the Woods Hole Oceanographic Institution. In 1950, William Schevill used underwater microphones, called hydrophones, to listen to sperm whales.

Schevill hoped to confirm reports he had heard from old whalers that sperm whales talked to each other beneath the surface of the water. The whalers thought the sperm whales were warning each other about the ship. Schevill suspected the clicks were a form of sonar, which later proved to be correct.[3]

▶ Setting Sail to Study Sperm Whales

By the 1970s, zoologists were studying several whale species, including humpback whales and right whales. However, most scientists thought sperm whales would be too difficult to study because they lived too far from land and spent too much time in the ocean depths.

In 1981, World Wildlife Fund Netherlands funded a research project aboard a thirty-three-foot (ten-meter) sloop named *Tulip*. Research designed to learn about the life and behavior of sperm

The Ocean Alliance is committed to the conservation of whales and their habitat. This site provides information on whale research, including the voyage of the *Odyssey*, a five-and-a-half-year expedition to study the effect of ocean pollution on marine life.

EDITOR'S CHOICE

Access this Web site from http://www.myreportlinks.com

whales began in earnest in 1982, when biologists Hal Whitehead and Jonathan Gordon took the *Tulip* to the Indian Ocean. There they used hydrophones to follow sperm whales for two years.

Since then, Whitehead, Gordon, and other zoologists have conducted research aboard ships to monitor whales in other parts of the ocean. Whitehead began a long-term study of sperm whales near the Galápagos Islands in 1985. In 1987 the International Fund for Animal Welfare purchased a yacht named *Song of the Whale* to study marine animals. The *Song of the Whale* crew, which included Gordon, studied sperm whales near the Azores, a group of nine islands off Portugal's coast, for many years.

In 1991 the Ocean Alliance received a donated ninety-three-foot (twenty-eight-meter) steel-hulled ketch named *Odyssey*. In 2005, the *Odyssey* completed a five-year study of ocean pollution. The *Odyssey* crew gathered extensive information about sperm whales around the world.

▶ Hydrophones

Finding and tracking an animal that spends so much time deep in the ocean is challenging. It would have been impossible if not for the development of underwater microphones called hydrophones. When combined in "arrays," or groups, hydrophones indicate the direction that whale clicks are coming from.

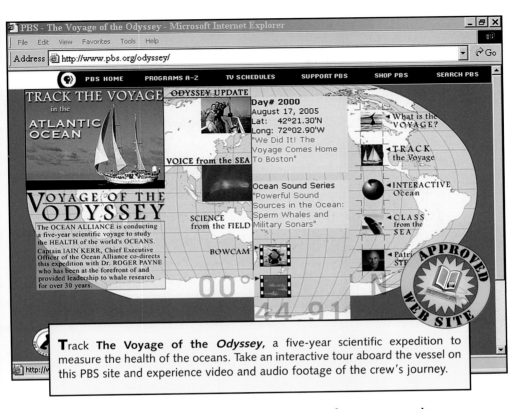

Track **The Voyage of the *Odyssey*,** a five-year scientific expedition to measure the health of the oceans. Take an interactive tour aboard the vessel on this PBS site and experience video and audio footage of the crew's journey.

The *Odyssey* towed two underwater microphones contained in a 30-foot (9-meter), oil-filled tube. These hydrophones picked up whale clicks that were 5 to 10 miles (8 to 16 kilometers) away. A computer program named Rainbow Click helped researchers analyze whale clicks to locate the whales. Rainbow Click also separated whale clicks, representing the clicks of different whales in different colors in its program.[4]

▷ Photoidentification

In order to count whales, researchers need to be able to tell one whale from another.

They also want to be able to recognize individual whales so they can monitor these whales over time. If researchers see a whale near the Galápagos Islands in March and then see the same whale near Mexico in June, they will have learned something about whale behavior. However, whales tend to look like unidentifiable logs when they rest at the surface.

There is one part of a sperm whale that is slightly different on each whale and is very visible

▽ A scientist working with the Stellwagen Bank National Marine Sanctuary places a D-tag on the back of a humpback whale in Sanctuary waters off the coast of Massachusetts. See page 98 for more information on D-tags.

for a moment or so about once an hour—the whale's flukes. The flukes are scalloped along the outside, and the pattern varies a little from whale to whale. In addition, distinct nicks, scars, and holes often mark the flukes.

Sperm whales begin a deep dive by lifting their flukes above the water. A photograph taken at the moment the flukes are in the air provides a sort of whale fingerprint.

▶ DNA Analysis

As whales move through the water, they leave behind sheets of their skin. They shed skin most often when they are socializing, as they rub against each other. Whales seem to enjoy rolling along the body of another whale. Shedding skin may be important for whales because underwater parasites cling to their skin.

Researchers traveling behind the whales can pick up these pieces of skin. If they are also taking photographs, they may even be able to match the skin to a photograph. The skin provides DNA, the material inside the nucleus of a cell that carries genetic information, which can be analyzed to determine if whales traveling together are related.

Researchers aboard the *Odyssey* used biopsy darts to obtain samples from whales. The dart was fired from a crossbow so that it hit a whale's back and then bounced off and floated in the water.

Once researchers retrieved the dart with a net, they took the dart with its little piece of skin and blubber to a sterile laboratory where it was divided into eight pieces for later analysis. Meanwhile someone else made notes about the whale the sample came from. *Odyssey* researchers were particularly interested in learning how much pollution was stored in the whale's blubber.[5]

▶ D-tags

In 1999, electronic engineers and biologists at the Woods Hole Oceanographic Institution worked together to develop the digital acoustic recording tag, or D-tag. The D-tag is a miniature computer, with as much as six gigabytes of memory, that records sound using hydrophones. The tag also contains a pressure sensor to measure the depth of a dive and both an orientation sensor and a pitch sensor to measure the whale's movements. One additional part, a tiny radio beacon, allows researchers to find the tag in the ocean.

In spite of all it contains, the tag is very small. It measures 4 by 1.5 by 1 inches (10 by 3.8 by 2.5 centimeters) and weighs about 5 ounces. All of the electronic parts can withstand the pressure deep in the ocean, and they are contained in a thick urethane bag.[6]

The tag is attached to the whale with a suction cup. While the tag is attached, it measures depth,

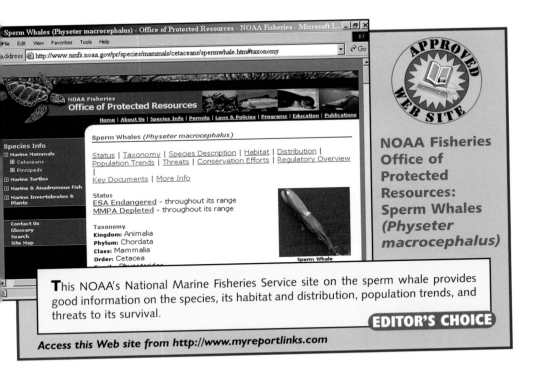

NOAA Fisheries
Office of
Protected
Resources:
Sperm Whales
(*Physeter
macrocephalus*)

This NOAA's National Marine Fisheries Service site on the sperm whale provides good information on the species, its habitat and distribution, population trends, and threats to its survival.

EDITOR'S CHOICE

Access this Web site from http://www.myreportlinks.com

sounds, movement, and temperature fifty times a second.[7] After about twelve hours, the tag falls off and floats on the ocean surface.

▷ Using the Tags

Researchers aboard the *Odyssey* used D-tags to obtain information about whale dives. However, initially sticking the tag on a whale required patience and nerve. A researcher had to get 25 feet (7.6 meters) out over the water on a long beam extending from the side of the boat. The boat then approached the whales as quietly as possible as the researcher attempted to place the suction cup with a long pole. For one study, researchers were able to stick only four tags on whales in forty-five attempts.[8]

When a biologist with Woods Hole used tags to monitor two or three whales at the same time, he found that the whales dive together and use codas to communicate at the beginning of their dive. They then stay a steady distance from each other and seem to be listening to each other's clicks. As they approach the surface, they again communicate with codas.[9]

▶ More Research

Governments, including the United States government, also conduct research to better understand whales. For example, since 1994, NOAA's National Marine Fisheries Service (NMFS) has prepared annual reports on the status of whales in the Atlantic Ocean, the Gulf of Mexico, and the Pacific Ocean. These reports include population estimates and trends, and deaths and injuries caused by fishing operations.

Chapter 6 ▶

USING RESEARCH TO HELP SPERM WHALES

Governments and nonprofit agencies are investing the time and resources to learn about sperm whales. Equipped with new technologies, researchers are adding new findings to the store of knowledge about these whales. But knowledge by itself is not the goal of researchers. The knowledge is meant to be the basis of specific actions that will help sperm whales thrive.

▶ The Question of Numbers

One important question remains unanswered: How many sperm whales live in the oceans? The answer is important for several reasons. One reason is simply that Japan would like to resume whaling. In the recent past, Japanese whalers have killed a few sperm whales each year for "scientific research." If Japan is able to gather enough votes to overturn the International Whaling Commission's moratorium on whaling, whaling ships may once again process greater numbers of sperm whales.

The IWC has already developed a Revised Management Plan for whaling, although this plan has not been implemented.[1] However, the existence of the Revised Management Plan indicates that the moratorium may not be permanent. History has already shown that commercial whaling is difficult to control.

Drift Net Ban

Research does lead to legislation and treaties to improve conditions for marine mammals. For example, as evidence piled up about the harmful effects of drift net fishing on marine mammals, countries around the world paid attention. In 1989, many countries agreed to ban or limit drift nets. By the end of 1989, the United Nations General Assembly unanimously adopted Resolution 44/225, which called for an end to drift net fishing on the high seas beginning in 1992.[2]

Drift nets still present a danger to marine mammals. Fishermen still use the nets illegally, and abandoned nets still float in the oceans. However, the moratorium has reduced the harm done by drift nets.

Ship Strikes on Whales

NOAA has paid attention to research about the number of whales killed because ships run into them. In 2004, the agency proposed rules to reduce the number of ship strikes and submitted the rules for public comment. The rules, which had not been enacted by 2006, include changing routes used by ships and imposing speed limits.[3] NOAA also uses aircraft to look for whales and then informs ships of whale locations.

These efforts are intended mostly to help northern right whales. These slow-swimming whales seem most likely to be hit by ships in waters off the eastern coast of the United States. However, rules and procedures adopted by the United States may serve as models for use in parts of the world where sperm whales are sometimes victims of ship strikes.

Ocean Pollution

Scientific findings leave no doubt that ocean pollution is a serious threat to marine life. The problem is complex, and solutions require international cooperation. International treaties and national laws chip away at the problem, but pollutants including toxic chemicals, sewage, and other waste materials continue to find their way to the ocean. And pollution from past decades is still there.

The first international treaty on ocean dumping, the London Convention of 1972, banned dumping of many toxic materials. A 1996 protocol, or amendment, to the London Convention widened its scope. The 1972 treaty listed what

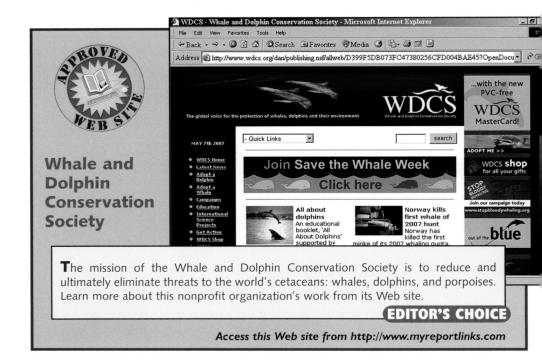

File   Edit   View   Favorites   Tools   Help

Back   ·   ·   Search   Favorites   Media

Address   http://www.wdcs.org/dan/publishing.nsf/allweb/D399F5DB073FC47380256CFD004BAE45?OpenDocu

...with the new
PVC-free
WDCS
MasterCard!

WDCS

The global voice for the protection of whales, dolphins and their environment   Whale and Dolphin Conservation Society

ADOPT ME >>

MAY 7th 2007

- Quick Links   search

WDCS **shop**
for all your gifts

Whale and
Dolphin
Conservation
Society

- WDCS Home
- Latest News
- Adopt a Dolphin
- Adopt a Whale
- Campaigns
- Education
- International Science Projects
- Get Active
- WDCS Shop

Join Save the Whale Week
Click here

STOP BLOODY WHALING

Join our campaign today
www.stopbloodywhaling.org

All about
dolphins
An educational
booklet, 'All
About Dolphins'
supported by

Norway kills
first whale of
2007 hunt
Norway has
killed the first
minke of its 2007 whaling quota.

out of the blue

The mission of the Whale and Dolphin Conservation Society is to reduce and ultimately eliminate threats to the world's cetaceans: whales, dolphins, and porpoises. Learn more about this nonprofit organization's work from its Web site.

EDITOR'S CHOICE

Access this Web site from http://www.myreportlinks.com

could not be dumped in the ocean. The 1996 amendment provides a list of what can be dumped, making the dumping of anything else illegal. This amendment became effective in 2006.

In recent decades, the International Maritime Organization (IMO), formed by the United Nations to increase ship safety, has turned its attention to ocean pollution as well. For example, IMO adopted the International Convention on the Control of Harmful Anti-fouling Systems on Ships, which makes it illegal for ships to use paints that pollute the ocean.[4] Other IMO conventions, or treaties, address pollution from ships and prevention of oil spills.

▶ Deadly Noise

There is no question that the ocean is a noisier place than it was a decade ago—and it is getting noisier. Man-made underwater noises include sonar, ship traffic, use of explosives, underwater construction, offshore oil drilling, and seismic testing for oil.

Many scientists and conservationists believe that the increased level of noise is harmful to fish and mammals that live in the ocean. Conservationists are especially concerned that the use of sonar in naval tests harms whales. In 2002, veterinary researchers examined a group of beaked whales that had died after a mass stranding in the Canary Islands, which lie in the Atlantic Ocean off the northwestern coast of Africa. The whales became stranded near the site of an international naval test. The stranding came only four hours after mid-frequency sonar activity had begun.

When the veterinary researchers examined the whales, they found internal bleeding around the whales' ears and brains and around the oil in their jaws that seems to transmit sound. The whales also had injuries similar to the injuries found in people suffering severe decompression sickness (also called "the bends") when a too-rapid decrease in air pressure releases nitrogen into the body's tissues.

The researchers believe the beaked whales died shortly after they became stranded and died

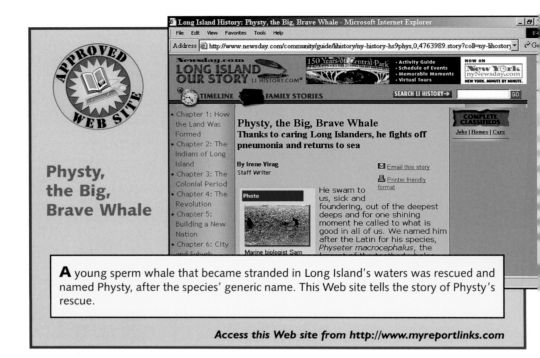

A young sperm whale that became stranded in Long Island's waters was rescued and named Physty, after the species' generic name. This Web site tells the story of Physty's rescue.

Access this Web site from http://www.myreportlinks.com

of heart failure, brought on by, in the researchers' words, "stranding stress syndrome."[5]

▷ The Noise Pollution Debate

The debate about whether loud man-made noises can kill or seriously harm marine mammals has led to research in this area. NOAA is working with universities, conservationists, and industries in an ongoing ocean acoustics program to monitor noise in the ocean.

Meanwhile, the World Conservation Union adopted a resolution in 2004 that calls on governments to stop causing loud noises in areas where the noises may affect marine mammals. The resolution urges governments to use the "precautionary principle" until more is known about the effects of noise pollution. It also calls for the development of new, less noisy technologies.[6] Noise pollution was also a topic of discussion at the 2006 United Nations Open-ended Informal Consultative Process of Oceans and the Law of the Sea.

Although the United States is the leader in producing ocean noise, the U.S. government chose not to participate in the IUCN discussion of noise pollution.

The Natural Resources Defense Council, an environmental organization, has taken the issue of noise pollution to the U.S. courts. One lawsuit, which the group won in 2003, led to restrictions on the use of the Navy's low-frequency active sonar system. A second lawsuit, brought to court in 2005, seeks restrictions on mid-frequency sonar.[7]

Inconclusive Research

So far, research about how noise pollution affects whales is not conclusive. Common sense tells us that so many loud noises would be harmful. However, scientists have observed whales continuing to hunt for food close to man-made noises. Some scientists believe the whales find less food in noisy environments, but they do not have the evidence to say for sure. Evidence about whether

▲ In this photo taken in the Gulf of Mexico, a sperm whale begins its dive near an oil-drilling rig. Scientists are concerned that the impact of man-made noise pollution may be detrimental to sperm whales.

loud man-made noises are causing hearing loss is also not conclusive.

▶ **Whale Watching**

Scientists are not the only people watching whales these days. Around the world, whale watching has become a moneymaking industry. Eighty-seven countries and overseas territories offer whale-watching tours that may last a few hours, days, or weeks. By 1998, people were spending more than one billion dollars per year to watch whales around the globe.[8] Conservationists hope that the whale-watching industry will make whales worth more alive than dead.

Whale watching began in California in the 1950s when people paid one dollar each to see gray whales. During the 1970s, boat owners in New England began offering tours to see humpback whales. Then, in the 1990s, the whale-watching industry began to grow rapidly. The number of people who paid to see whales increased by 12 percent per year through the decade.[9]

▷ The New Whalers

In some areas, men who once pursued whales to kill them now watch for whales to show them to people who want to learn more about them. The Azores exported tons of sperm whale oil after Yankee whalers brought whaling to the islands. Because the islands of the Azores are actually the tips of underwater mountains, the water around them is very deep, and sperm whales often come quite close to land. Hunting for sperm whales near the Azores ended in 1987.

Today, boats carry tourists instead of harpooners. Once again, *vigias* (lookouts) scan the horizon for the low, angled blow of the sperm whale. These days, though, they often use hydrophones as well as their eyes to locate the whales. And when the vigias spot whales, the boats carrying tourists approach them carefully so as not to frighten them.

The island of Dominica in the Caribbean also offers opportunities to see sperm whales. Like the Azores, Dominica is surrounded by very deep water, which sperm whales prefer. Research indicates that groups of females and juvenile sperm whales visit these waters year-round, but the best chances of seeing them are in the winter months, between November and March.

Kaikoura, New Zealand, and Andenes, Norway, offer opportunities to see large male sperm whales living in colder waters near the poles.

▷ Researchers and Whale Watching

Researchers contribute to the whale-watching industry in several ways, and local whale-watching businesses can sometimes help researchers gather information. For example, Jonathan Gordon, who has been collecting data about sperm whales for decades, helped establish whale-watching in Dominica. Like many conservationists, Gordon hopes to make living sperm whales economically valuable.

Knowledge about sperm whales has helped whale-watching industries develop rules to make whale watching safe for the whales as well as the watchers. There are no internationally enforced

The Sea Shepherd Conservation Society was founded more than thirty years ago by Canadian Paul Watson, an original member of Greenpeace. Read about the organization's work on the seas trying to enforce protections for whales and other marine mammals.

Access this Web site from http://www.myreportlinks.com

rules in the whale-watching industry, although the International Whaling Commission's scientific committee developed guidelines in 1996 to encourage whale watching that does not harm whales.

Some countries have laws to protect the whales. In other countries, rules are generally accepted although not legally enforced. In a few areas, no rules govern the operators of whale-watching tours.

▷ Whale-Watching Guidelines

Most whale-watching regulations are based on the IWC guidelines. These guidelines state that boats should be operated in such a way as to minimize noise and sudden changes in noise. This guideline is especially important for sperm whales because, as the Yankee whalers noticed, they seem to be especially sensitive to sound. Even small noises can startle the huge animals if the noises are unexpected.

Engine noise might also interfere with the whales' communication. The whales rely on hearing the echoes of their clicks for navigation, and they seem to communicate with one another regularly.

The IWC guidelines also state that the whales should govern the "visit." For example, if whales seem unhappy about being watched, they should be allowed to leave. Boats should never surround or chase the whales. While boats should be quiet, they should not sneak up on the whales silently and surprise them. Sperm whales are shy and seem frightened when they suddenly notice that a boat is very close.

Some countries state specifically at what distance from whales the whale-watching boats must stop. Responsible boat operators know enough about the whales to recognize when the boat is disturbing them.

▶ Sperm Whales and Whale Watchers

Whale watching can disturb whales in many ways. For example, sperm whales seem to need about ten minutes of recovery time between their deep dives. During this time at the surface, they need to replenish the oxygen in their bodies. Researchers have noticed that whales approached by whale watchers spend less time at the surface, which may mean they are not able to spend as much time diving.

Some boat operators may see a sperm whale's blow and hurry toward it to catch a glimpse before it disappears from view. Doing so can cause the whale to slip under water before it is ready for a deep dive. Because they spend so little time at the surface, sperm whales may seem to be a poor choice for whale watchers.

The use of hydrophones, though, can make watching sperm whales rewarding. Boat operators can locate the whales underwater and be close— but not too close—when they come to the surface. People can then watch the whales at the surface and see the huge flukes lifted high as the whales dive. When hydrophones are connected to the boat's speaker system, passengers can listen to the whales' clicks as the whales hunt and as they communicate.

▶ Who Are the Whales?

While facts and figures tell us about sperm whales and the world they live in, sperm whale expert Hal Whitehead hopes research will help people feel they know whales personally. He wonders, for example, how whales see their lifelong companions. Do they see individuals with personalities and desires? Why did whales stay with wounded companions during whaling years when that loyalty meant death? Did they simply not know any better, or did they, in a real sense, care for other members of their species?

Whitehead has pointed out that researchers studying gorillas and chimpanzees feel that they get insights into the minds of these animals. Their work provides us with knowledge and pictures that bring the animals to life for us. However, the world of the sperm whale is new to humans. It is difficult for us to imagine "seeing" the world through the echoes it sends back or being on the move all the time in the vast oceans.

Are sperm whale codas nothing more than patterns of sound that identify individuals? Or are they a form of language?

New technologies that allow researchers to listen in on deep dives and to identify the clicks of individual whales promise exciting results. A database of photographs that allows researchers to study individual whales over time should also provide a clearer picture of the lives of whales. Eventually the knowledge scientists gain may help them see the world from a whale's point of view. Until then, we can all play an important part by protecting these mysterious deep-sea dwellers and their habitat so they do not disappear from the earth's oceans forever.

In 1973, Congress took the farsighted step of creating the Endangered Species Act, widely regarded as the world's strongest and most effective wildlife conservation law. It set an ambitious goal: to reverse the alarming trend of human-caused extinction that threatened the ecosystems we all share.

Each book in this series explores the life of an endangered animal. The books tell how and why the animals have become endangered and explain the efforts being made to restore their populations.

The United States Fish and Wildlife Service and the National Marine Fisheries Service share responsibility for administration of the Endangered Species Act. Over time, animals are added to, reclassified in, or removed from the federal list of Endangered and Threatened Wildlife and Plants. At the time of publication, all the animals in this series were listed as endangered species. The most up-to-date list can be found at **http://www.fws.gov/endangered/wildlife.html**.

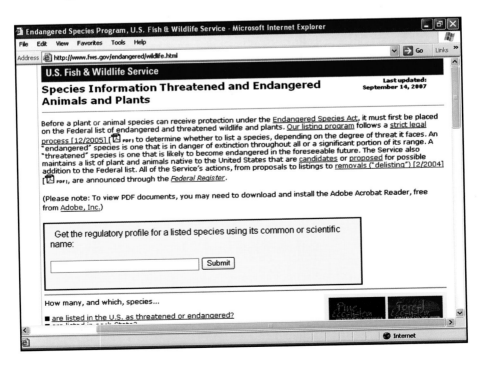

Report Links

The Internet sites described below can be accessed at
http://www.myreportlinks.com

▶**Woods Hole Oceanographic Institution**
Editor's Choice Learn more about the science of oceans when you visit this Web site.

▶**ARKive: Sperm Whale (Physeter macrocephalus)**
Editor's Choice An online database features images of endangered animals, including the sperm wh

▶**NOAA Fisheries Office of Protected Resources: Sperm Whales (Physeter macrocephal**
Editor's Choice NOAA offers an overview of sperm whales on this site.

▶**Whale and Dolphin Conservation Society**
Editor's Choice The Whale and Dolphin Conservation Society protects cetaceans.

▶**Ocean Alliance**
Editor's Choice Learn about the state of the world's oceans from this Web site.

▶***Nature:* "Sperm Whales—The Real Moby Dick"**
Editor's Choice This PBS site provides a look at the real species portrayed in Melville's famous no

▶**Battle of the Titans**
This *National Wildlife* magazine article takes a look at sperm whales and giant squid.

▶**Cetacean Society International**
Take an online tour of cetaceans at this site.

▶**Discovering Whales: The Sperm Whale**
Whales on the Net provides an in-depth look at sperm whales.

▶**Eight European States Hit With Legal Action Over Whale Protection**
Learn how fishing practices are hurting whales and other species.

▶**The International Whaling Commission**
Learn about the International Whaling Commission from its Web site.

▶**Keep America Beautiful**
Learn how to reduce pollution and waste in your own backyard.

▶**The Life and Works of Herman Melville**
Learn about *Moby Dick's* creator from this Web site.

▶**Modern Whaling**
A brief history of modern whaling is presented by this site.

▶**Monterey Bay Aquarium: Seafood Watch Program**
An aquarium site offers consumers the chance to make environmentally wise choices when buying fis

Report Links

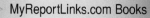

The Internet sites described below can be accessed at http://www.myreportlinks.com

▶**The National Marine Mammal Laboratory Education Site**
Learn about marine mammals, including sperm whales, and careers in marine science.

▶**New Bedford Whaling Museum**
Visit the virtual home of the largest whaling museum in the United States.

▶**NOAA National Marine Sanctuaries**
A national program of sanctuaries is saving whales and other marine mammals.

▶**The Oceania Project**
This organization is dedicated to raising awareness about whales and related species.

▶***Physeter macrocephalus***
View the IUCN Red List data for sperm whales.

▶**Physty, the Big, Brave Whale**
Read a news story about a sick sperm whale that got stranded.

▶**Sea Shepherd Conservation Society**
A conservation organization sets sail to save whales and other marine mammals.

▶**Sound Science**
This Web site presents recent research on how sound affects animals and fish.

▶**Sperm Whale Cetacean Info**
Hear the clicks, codas, and other sounds made by sperm whales.

▶**Sperm Whale Research in Northern Norway**
This Whale and Dolphin Conservation Society page looks at sperm whale research in Norway.

▶**Spying on Leviathan**
The National Wildlife Federation examines the Sperm Whale Seismic Study (SWSS).

▶**Tracking Sperm Whales and Jumbo Squid**
For the first time, sperm whales and jumbo squid are tagged together.

▶**USFWS Endangered Species Program Kid's Corner**
This USFWS Web site offers ways you can help save endangered species.

▶**The Voyage of the *Odyssey***
Learn about an epic scientific journey to study the effects of ocean pollution on marine species.

▶**Whale Vomit Sparks Cash Bonanza**
This BBC News article discusses the value of ambergris.

ambergris—A waxy substance, thought to be produced by sperm whales in their intestines, that is often found floating on the surface of the sea or washed up on beaches. As the substance ages, it develops a sweet, earthy aroma. Once valued for its use in perfumes, such use is illegal today.

baleen—Long strips of a bony substance called keratin that hang from the roof of a baleen whale's mouth instead of teeth. Baleen acts as a filter, trapping food in and expelling water.

baleen whales—Whales that have baleen plates instead of teeth so they can filter food from the water. Blue whales and right whales are among the many species of baleen whales.

bioluminescence—Light given off by a living organism. Fireflies are bioluminescent as are some fish living deep in the ocean.

blowhole—A hole on the left side of sperm whales' heads through which they breathe air. When sperm whales exhale, they produce an angled "bushy" blow, or spout, that might rise 15 feet (5 meters) in the air. Baleen whales have two blowholes.

blubber—A thick layer of fat covering the bodies of sperm whales and other cetaceans. Blubber stores energy and provides insulation.

Cetacea—The scientific name for the order of marine mammals that includes whales, dolphins, and porpoises.

codas—Patterns of sperm whale clicks that sound a little like Morse code. Sperm whales may use codas to communicate.

dorsal fin—The triangular fin on the back of sperm whales, other cetaceans, and fishes. The dorsal fin helps cetaceans and fishes to swim straight without rolling to the side. Sperm whales' dorsal fins are low and squat as compared with the tall dorsal fins of orcas.

echolocation—A way of "seeing" in the dark by listening to echoes. Sperm whales click and then listen to the echoes of the clicks to navigate and find food in the dark ocean depths.

flukes—The two triangular fins on whales' tails. Sperm whale flukes may be up to 16 feet (5 meters) across.

global warming—The increase in Earth's temperature, including the oceans. Increased amounts of carbon dioxide and other gases resulting from human activities may be causing temperatures to increase, which has already begun to affect glacial melting, food supplies, and ocean depths.

moratorium—A pause in an activity or an end to that activity.

odontocetes—The group of whales, including sperm whales, that have teeth. They are also called toothed whales.

render—The term used for cooking whale blubber to extract the oil.

rorqual—The name given to a group of baleen whales. The word is Norwegian for "grooved whale." Rorqual whales have pleats along their throats and bellies that enable them to expand their throats to swallow huge amounts of ocean water containing small ocean creatures. Rorqual whales are graceful in motion (even the 150-ton [136 metric tons] blue whale) and can swim very fast.

sonar—An acronym for "**so**und **na**vigation **r**anging." Sonar uses echolocation to find objects in the water.

tryworks—Brick furnaces on whaling ships of the 1800s. Whale blubber was rendered in huge iron pots in the furnace.

Chapter 1. Sperm Whales in Danger

1. "The Wreck of the Whaleship Essex," *BBC,* n.d., <http://www.bbc.co.uk/dna/h2g2/alabaster/A671492> (September 4, 2006).

2. Herman Melville, *Moby Dick* (New York: The Modern Library, 1992), p. 92.

3. "Rock Art Hints at Whaling Origins," *BBC News.com,* Tuesday, April 20, 2004, <http://news.bbc.co.uk/2/hi/science/nature/3638853.stm> (April 16, 2007).

4. "Overview of American Whaling," *New Bedford Whaling Museum,* n.d., <http://www.whalingmuseum.org/kendall/amwhale/am_index.html> (August 25, 2006).

5. "Whaling," *The History Channel,* n.d., <http://www.history.com/encyclopedia. do?articleId=225766> (September 6, 2006).

6. Richard Ellis, *The Empty Ocean* (Washington, D.C.: Island Press, 2003), p. 248.

7. Hal Whitehead, *Sperm Whales: Social Evolution in the Ocean* (Chicago: The University of Chicago Press, 2003), p. 20.

8. "City Mayors: US cities population in 2005," *City Mayors,* n.d., <http://www.citymayors.com/statistics/us_cities_population.html> (September 23, 2006).

9. "Problems: Ocean Pollution," *World Wildlife Fund,* n.d., <http://www.panda.org/about_wwf/what_we_do/marine/problems/pollution/index.cfm> (August 26, 2006).

Chapter 2. Hunters in the Ocean Depths

1. Hal Whitehead, *Sperm Whales: Social Evolution in the Ocean* (Chicago: The University of Chicago Press, 2003), p. xix.

2. Ibid., p. 9.

3. Jonathan Gordon, *Sperm Whales* (Stillwater, Minn.: Voyageur Press, Inc., 1998), p. 11.

4. Roger Payne, "Noise Pollution: Part 1," *PBS: The Voyage of the Odyssey: Voice from the Sea,* June 28, 2002, <http://www.pbs.org/odyssey/voice/20020628_vfts_transcript.html> (May 21, 2007).

5. Bijal P. Trivedi, "Sperm Whale 'Voices' Used to Gauge Whales' Sizes," *National Geographic News,* November 3, 2003, <http://news.nationalgeographic.com/news/2003/11/1103_031103_tvspermwhale.html> (June 22, 2006).

6. Gordon, p. 12.

7. "Sperm Whale Fact Sheet," *Ocean Alliance,* n.d., <http://www.oceanalliance.org/education/spermwhale_facts.html> (September 6, 2006).

8. Genevieve Johnson, "Deep Divers and the Bends," *PBS: The Voyage of the Odyssey: Track the Voyage: The Maldives,* January 28, 2003, <http://www.pbs.org/odyssey/odyssey/20030128_log_transcript.html> (September 6, 2006).

9. Genevieve Johnson, "The Diving Physiology of the Sperm Whale," *PBS: The Voyage of the Odyssey: Track the Voyage: Papua New Guinea,* May 31, 2001, <http://www.pbs.org/odyssey/odyssey/20010606_log_transcript.html> (September 6, 2006).

10. Whitehead, p. 60.

11. John Pickrell, "Fossils Show How Whales Evolved to Hear Underwater," *National Geographic News,* August 11, 2004, <http://news.nationalgeographic.com/news/2004/08/0811_040811_whale_evolution.html> (June 22, 2006).

12. Genevieve Johnson, "The Evolution of Whales," *PBS: The Voyage of the Odyssey: Track the Voyage: Australia,* December 17, 2001, <http://www.pbs.org/odyssey/odyssey/20011217_log_transcript.html> (August 23, 2006).

13. Whitehead, p. 100.

14. Ibid., p. 140.

15. Benjamin Kahn, "The Acoustic Realm of the Sperm Whale—Part I," *PBS: The Voyage of the Odyssey: Track the Voyage: Papua New Guinea,* March 15, 2001, <http://www.pbs.org/odyssey/odyssey/20010315_log_transcript.html> (August 23, 2006).

16. Whitehead, p. 323.

17. Ibid., pp. 184–185.

18. Gordon, p. 25.

Chapter 3. Dangers of the Deep

1. "Overview of American Whaling," *New Bedford Whaling Museum,* n.d., <http://www.whalingmuseum.org/kendall/amwhale/am_index.html> (August 25, 2006).

2. "How Whales Were Captured," *New Bedford Whaling Museum,* n.d., <http://www.whalingmuseum.org/kendall/amwhale/am_captured.html> (August 25, 2006).

3. "The Whaleboat," *New Bedford Whaling Museum,* n.d., <http://www.whalingmuseum.org/kendall/amwhale/am_whaleboat.html> (August 25, 2006).

4. "How Whales Were Captured," *New Bedford Whaling Museum.*

5. "How Whales Were Processed," *New Bedford Whaling Museum,* n.d., <http://www.whalingmuseum.org/kendall/amwhale/am_processed.html> (August 25, 2006).

6. "ACS Sperm Whale Cetacean Fact Sheet," *American Cetacean Society,* n.d., <http://www.acsonline.org/factpack/spermwhl.htm> (August 21, 2006).

7. Richard Ellis, *The Empty Ocean* (Washington, D.C.: Island Press, 2003), p. 249.

8. Hal Whitehead, *Sperm Whales: Social Evolution in the Ocean* (Chicago: The University of Chicago Press, 2003), p. 361.

9. Ibid., p. 362.

10. "The IUCN Red List of Threatened Species: *Physeter macrocephalus,*" *IUCN,* n.d., <http://www.redlist.org/search/details.php ?species=41755&tab=summ> (June 15, 2006).

11. "Background: Convention on the Prevention of Marine Pollution by Dumping of Wastes and Other Matter, 1972," *London Convention 1972,* n.d., <http://www.londonconvention.org/London_Convention .htm#Summary> (September 6, 2006).

12. Ibid.

13. "Pollution and Toxics," *WWF: Whale Watching in the Arctic,* n.d., <http:www.ngo.grida.no/wwfap/whalewatching/threats_pollution .shtml> (July 7, 2006).

14. Whitehead, p. 365.

15. Genevieve Johnson, "Disentangling Sperm Whales from Drift nets," *PBS: The Voyage of the Odyssey,* October 22, 2004, <http://www .pbs.org/odyssey/odyssey/20041022_log_transcript.html> (July 4, 2006).

16. Ibid.

17. Whitehead, p. 364.

Chapter 4. Protection for Whales

1. Angela Lang, "Detailed Discussion: The Global Protection of Whales," *Michigan State University College of Law: Animal Legal & Historical Web Center,* 2002, <http://www.animallaw.info/articles /dduswhales.htm> (July 4, 2006).

2. Richard Ellis, *The Empty Ocean* (Washington, D.C.: Island Press, 2003), p. 251.

3. "NOAA Fisheries Service Seeks Comments on Sperm Whale Recovery Plan," *National Oceanic & Atmospheric Administration: U.S. Department of Commerce,* July 6, 2006, <http://www.nmfs.noaa.gov /pr/pdfs/recovery/draft_spermwhale.pdf> (September 7, 2006).

4. Lang.

5. Ibid.

6. Ibid.

7. "Revenge of the Whale Hunters," *Time,* July 3, 2006, vol. 168, no. 1.

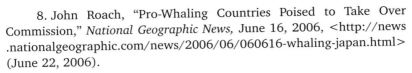
8. John Roach, "Pro-Whaling Countries Poised to Take Over Commission," *National Geographic News,* June 16, 2006, <http://news .nationalgeographic.com/news/2006/06/060616-whaling-japan.html> (June 22, 2006).

9. Lang.

Chapter 5. The Work of Researchers

1. Hal Whitehead, *Sperm Whales: Social Evolution in the Ocean* (Chicago: The University of Chicago Press, 2003), p. 375.

2. Ibid., p. 102.

3. "The Chattering Whale," *Time,* August 19, 1957, <http://www.time .com/time/magazine/printout/0,8816,809763,00.html> (September 2, 2006).

4. Roger Payne, "How We Find and Track Sperm Whales," *PBS: The Voyage of the Odyssey,* December 22, 2000, <http:www.pbs.org /odyssey/20001222_log_transcript.html> (August 23, 2006).

5. Roger Payne, "The Science of the Voyage—Collecting Biopsy Samples from Sperm Whales," *PBS: The Voyage of the Odyssey,* December 22, 2000, <http://www.pbs.org/odyssey/odyssey/20040324_log_ transcript.html> (October 13, 2006).

6. Mark P. Johnson, "Playing Tag With Whales," *Oceanus: The Online Magazine of Research From Woods Hole Oceanographic Institution,* n.d., <http://www.whoi.edu/oceanus/printArticle.do?id=3820> (September 2, 2006).

7. Peter Tyack, "Run Deep, But Not Silent," *Oceanus: The Online Magazine of Research From Woods Hole Oceanographic Institution,* n.d., <http://www.whoi.edu/oceanus/printArticle.do?id=3818> (September 2, 2006).

8. P. T. Madsen, et al, "Sperm Whale Sound Production Studied With Ultrasound Time/Depth-Recording Tags," *PBS: The Voyage of the Odyssey,* April 2002, <http://www.pbs.org/odyssey/voyage/oa_jeb _spermtags.pdf> (August 21, 2006).

9. Tyack.

Chapter 6. Using Research to Help Sperm Whales

1. "IWC Information," *International Whaling Commission,* n.d., <http://www.iwcoffice.org/commission/iwcmain.htm#conservation> (October 13, 2006).

2. "International Law Governing Drift net Fishing on the High Seas," *Earth Trust,* n.d., <http://www.earthtrust.org/dnpaper/intllaw.html> (September 4, 2006).

3. "Federal Registrar/Vol. 71, No. 122," *NOAA Fisheries Office of Protected Resources,* 2006, <http://www.nmfs.noaa.gov/pr/pdfs/fr/fr71 -36299.pdf> (June 26, 2006).

4. "International Convention on the Control of Harmful Anti-fouling Systems on Ships," *International Maritime Organization,* n.d., <http://www.imo.org/Conventions/mainframe.asp?topic_id=529> (September 7, 2006).

5. A. Fernández, J.F. Edwards, et al, "Gas and Fat Embolic Syndrome Involving a Mass Stranding of Beaked Whales (Family *Ziphiidae*) Exposed to Anthropogenic Sonar Signals," *Veterinary Pathology,* American College of Veterinary Pathologists, vol. 42, 2005, pp. 446–457, <http://www.vetpathology.org/cgi/content/full/42/4/ 446> (April 18, 2007).

6. "World Conservation Union (IUCN) Adopts Resolution on Undersea Noise," *Animals in the Ocean,* November 2004, <http:// www.awionline.org/whales/news/IUCN_Resolution_on_Noise.htm> (September 7, 2006).

7. "Navy Sued Over Harm to Whales From Mid-Frequency Sonar," *NRDC Press Archive,* October 19, 2005, <http://www.nrdc.org/media /pressreleases/051019.asp> (October 11, 2006).

8. "Documenting the Growth of the Whale-Watching Industry," *IFAW,* n.d., <http://www.ifaw.org/ifaw/general/default.aspx?oid=10196> (November 15, 2006).

9. Ibid.

Further Reading

Billinghurst, Jane, ed. *The Spirit of the Whale: Legend, History, Conservation.* Stillwater, Minn.: Voyageur Press, 2000.

Collard, Sneed B. *A Whale Biologist at Work.* New York: Franklin Watts, 2001.

Currie, Stephen. *Thar She Blows: American Whaling in the Nineteenth Century.* Minneapolis: Lerner Publications, 2001.

Hoyt, Erich. *Whale Rescue: Changing the Future for Endangered Wildlife.* Buffalo: Firefly Books, 2005.

Littlefield, Cindy A. *Awesome Ocean Science! Investigating the Secrets of the Underwater World.* Charlotte, Vt.: Williamson Publishing, 2003.

McCutcheon, Scott, and Bobbi McCutcheon. *The Facts on File Marine Science Handbook.* New York: Facts on File, 2003.

O'Hara, Megan, ed. *A Whaling Captain's Daughter: The Diary of Laura Jernegan, 1868–1871.* Mankato, Minn.: Blue Earth Books, 2000.

Philbrick, Nathaniel. *Revenge of the Whale: The True Story of the Whaleship Essex.* New York: G.P. Putnam, 2002.

Pringle, Laurence. *Whales! Strange and Wonderful.* Honesdale, Pa.: Boyds Mills Press, 2003.

Sandler, Martin W. *Trapped in Ice: An Amazing True Whaling Adventure.* New York: Scholastic Nonfiction, 2006.

Fiction

Melville, Herman. *Moby Dick. Or, The Whale.* With an introduction by Nathaniel Philbrick. New York: Penguin, 2001. Also available online: Moby Dick by Herman Melville, *Project Gutenberg,* <http://www.gutenberg.org/etext/15>.